EMBROIDERED
PORTRAITS

EMBROIDERED PORTRAITS

IDEAS, INSPIRATION AND TECHNIQUES

JAN MESSENT

SEARCH PRESS

First published in Great Britain 2012

Search Press Limited
Wellwood, North Farm Road,
Tunbridge Wells, Kent TN2 3DR

Text copyright © Jan Messent 2012

Photographs by Roddy Paine Photographic Studios

Photographs and design copyright
© Search Press Ltd 2012

ISBN: 978-1-84448-741-7

Suppliers

For details of suppliers, please visit the Search Press
website: www.searchpress.com.

Acknowledgements

Once again I am indebted to Search Press for
giving me the opportunity to indulge myself
at their expense in subjects that fascinate
me, combining history, portraits, fashion and
embroidery all in one. Thank you to Roz Dace
and Katie Sparkes, my editors, for making the
process so pleasurable, and for involving me
at every stage. However, the book would not
be nearly so beautiful without the expertise
of Gavin Sawyer, the photographer who
understands how to hide the flaws as well as
how to bring out the best bits. Thank you to all
the team, and to my loving family who give me
space, peace, and comfort to work in.

Jan Messent. Hampshire. 2012.

Printed in Malaysia

CONTENTS

INTRODUCTION 8

A SHORT HISTORY OF EMBROIDERED PORTRAITS 10

THE FACE 16

THE BASIC HEAD 18

PAINTED FACES AND STITCHED HAIR-STYLES 24

ANNE OF CLEVES 34

PADDED HEADS IN PROFILE 38

WHITE EDWARDIAN LADY 42

THREE-QUARTER HEADS 46

BESS OF HARDWICKE 54

APPLIQUÉ HANDS 56

STITCHES FOR HAIR 58

WIGS 66

USING FELT 70

FABRICS LESS LIKELY TO FRAY 76

CLOTHING THE PORTRAIT 78

BASIC GARMENTS IN PROFILE 86

POSTCARD PORTRAITS 88

ONCE UPON A TIME 92

STITCHES 96

INSPIRATION 100

POSTCARD BOOK 116

INDEX 128

Fabric was used here to frame drawings from the 1820s and 1830s, forming part of my postcard book (see page 125).

My interpretation of Cinderella, shown here in close-up, and of Prince Charming, is explored on pages 92–93.

INTRODUCTION

Anyone who embroiders will have realised how styles, subjects and techniques change over the years and often come full circle, more regularly now than previously because of new technology and the availability of tools, patterns, materials, books and tuition. This is good: there is room and to spare for every style, frivolous or serious, and for any technique, however obscure.

As for the subject matter, the human figure has never quite been out of fashion, although it came rather close during the 'Jacobean crewelwork' era when writhing plants and animal forms covered every curtain and bedspread. The popularity of raised work balanced this with humans everywhere and now this seventeenth-century technique is in full swing once again, translating perfectly into twenty-first-century versions. To embroiderers, the clothes appear to present few problems, even the most intricate pieces, but the faces prove for the most part to be less successful, often not receiving the amount of attention they demand as the (arguably) most important element of any figure. So it is this most interesting of subjects that I have chosen to explore in greater detail than usual, and to share with you some methods that can be utilised in any kind of embroidery, not just in raised work in which special stitches are called for; these are not dealt with here.

My aim is to produce convincing heads and faces, male or female, mostly in appliqué of one kind or another, all realistic in style rather than whimsical or cutesy, and none of them with legs that show. Nor are any of my portraits doing anything but sitting still for the portraitist or photographer, wearing their best hair-dos, best hats and clothes, even best expressions. As for hands, those most troublesome of body parts, I have suggested a way of coping with these that differs from the usual 'wire-claw' effect. I hope you will approve of it, and make your own developments.

Just some of the embroideries that are included elsewhere in the book.

A SHORT HISTORY OF EMBROIDERED PORTRAITS

In an attempt to find something significant to say about portraiture in embroidery, my first discovery was that the subject does not fit neatly into centuries, eras or fashions in the same way that some other genres do. Leaving aside the many complex reasons why embroidery has been associated with women more than with men (not forgetting the Opus Anglicanum workshops of the early Middle Ages), it seems that figures have appeared in almost every phase of our embroidering history and that some of them were intended to represent recognisable characters, which one could argue makes them portraits as opposed to merely motifs. It also becomes clear that although the very first examples of embroidered faces are simplified almost to the point of abstraction, the works of subsequent eras from the tenth to the twenty-first centuries change in style rather than in excellence of drawing or technique. As an illustration of this, compare the exquisite workmanship and design of the Durham Vestments produced in *c.*905–910 by Winchester nuns with, for example, a picture of the infant Prince of Wales of *c.*1845 worked in Berlin woolwork to a professionally drawn design. To repeat, it is the designs and functions that appear to have changed much more than any development in skill. In this respect, embroidery is not unlike painting.

During the periods when professional embroiderers produced pieces for wealthy clients, for royalty and high ecclesiastics, the standard of both technique and design reached the highest levels, much of which can still be seen in museums and in large estates where church embroidery was hidden away during times of religious change. Many of these pieces depict Nativity scenes and saints finely worked in silk and gold thread, portraits so expressive and beautifully drawn that there is still nothing to better them today. Yet at the same time, we have other very early figurative pieces, also professionally designed, worked mostly by skilled amateurs to a tighter time schedule and with coarser materials to fulfill a completely different purpose. I refer specifically to the Bayeux Tapestry, embroidered by some of the same nuns who produced the famous goldwork, plus many other skilled noble refugees who flocked into their Wessex convents after the Norman Conquest of 1066. Materials, skill, design, function and time make all the difference to the quality of the finished product. And commitment too, no doubt. The embroiderers would not have been paid by Odo, Bishop of Bayeux, who commissioned it, and although it is still a marvellous testament to those women, it cannot compare in beauty to the famed goldwork of the same period.

Over the centuries, a wide variety of techniques has been employed on figurative embroidery to conform to the trends of each particular era, as will be seen from the few illustrations included here, with resulting successes and failures. Some less-than-perfect results are inevitably as much to do with unsympathetic treatment as with the draughtsmanship which, in most cases, was the work of itinerant professional artists who either were employed by the household as live-in designers or produced pattern books for anyone to use. With the latter, it is fascinating to note the repetition of motifs, particularly royal and biblical figures, on every household article that could be embroidered, resulting in some lively interpretations that obviously gave free rein to the imaginations of younger users. Some of these embroiderers would have been no more than eleven years old, yet the care they took over the task implies not only an astonishing tenacity, but also enjoyment. 'Mama, today I embroidered a caterpillar, and tomorrow I shall do King Charles' lace collar.' Needless to say, King Charles' lace collar, his hair and features took on a different aspect with each embroiderer. Not to mention the caterpillar. The Stuart monarchs, in embroidery, have left us with a rich legacy of ideas for the interpretation of our own later portraits, as have *Solomon and Sheba*, *David and Bathsheba*, and the *Five Senses*, among others.

The art of painting with stitches flourished in the Georgian period when women's artistic talents found a more acceptable (to men, that is) outlet in the copying of painted portraits by famous artists. There is a well-known 1779 self-portrait stitched in wool of a Mrs Knowles actually embroidering a portrait by Zoffany of George III, now in the Victoria and Albert Museum, London. Other talented women of the early nineteenth

Detail from a large hanging, the figure of Penelope, from Hardwicke Hall, Derbyshire, one of five great appliqué embroideries that dominated the State Withdrawing Chamber in 1601, at the end of Queen Elizabeth I's reign. Probably drawn by a professional artist, the flesh parts are covered with plain silk and embroidered in stem and back stitch.

Detail from a long cushion made for Hardwicke Hall, Derbyshire. The fine canvaswork figures and motifs have been applied to a black velvet background, worked with silk and metal threads. Seventeenth century.

This face detail is taken from the lid of an embroidered box made at the end of the seventeenth century. The satin skin is lightly padded and embroidered with silk, the hair worked in looped purl, as are many other parts of the scene. Bullion knots would create a similar effect. Victoria and Albert Museum, London.

century followed suit with depictions of their heroes, particularly Nelson and Bonaparte, worked in worsted threads on firm linen. Similar memorial panels were produced by American embroiderers in mourning for loved ones, worked in silk and gold, often designed and drawn out by local artists who, in some cases, also painted the faces.

As in England, there was a real need for women to express their losses and heartbreaks through the medium of therapeutic embroidery, and although it is easy at first to dismiss these pictures as overtly sentimental, it should be remembered that, for many women, death visited often and at a very early age, and there were few acceptable methods of coping with such frequent tragedies. Then, as now, embroidery was used as a means of self-expression and natural creativity, flourishing as communal projects during the periods after the wars in the making of altar frontals and banners for churches and societies on which portraits often played a central role.

Before this, the enthusiasm of William Morris for textiles gave rise to a painterly style of sentimental figurative work, mostly on woven tapestries, which failed to have quite the influence he would have liked on embroidery in general. Since then, the development of design and techniques has fostered a widespread interest in the medium as women, and some men, have recognised the potential in the use of fabric and stitch, macramé and lace, knitting and crochet as a valid artistic addition to painting. Indeed, many of today's professional embroiderers began their training in the fine arts, changing part-way from paint to textiles. Nowadays, figurative designs and those based on aspects of the human face are common, especially large-scale projects made to celebrate the year 2000 by village communities in which figures abound. Portraits rendered in Bayeux stitch, this time with less pressure, can be seen in parts of the amazing Quaker Tapestry. Elsewhere, every technique that was used in previous years, including *or nué*, raised work, blackwork and canvaswork, has been updated to new styles of portraiture that stretch the limitations of the materials and stitches to new boundaries.

Machine embroidery has also been responsible for a new flowering of experimentation, as has the use of computers for design and stitchery, the limitations of which are more in the hands of the operator than in the technology. There is still no substitute for recording observations with pencil and paper and, although a camera is a good aid, the art of study and sketch will always single out a competent designer from a mediocre one, in the past just as it does today. At the same time, even a superficial study of historic embroidered portraits will produce some excellent ideas for contemporary works, as the illustrations in this book will show. And although my portraits tend to be costume figures, because that is my interest, there is plenty of room for more contemporary interpretations in any setting, domestic or fanciful, just like those of earlier embroiderers.

I make no apologies for the fact that my examples are all made by hand, not machine, but this is not to say that the machine has no part in these experiments. On the contrary, I hope my suggestions will be utilised in any way that is convenient to you, scaled up, scaled down, whatever. The main aim is to enjoy yourself.

The portraits shown opposite are described in detail on the following pages.

John the Baptist, from part of the Durham Vestments, made in the tenth century by nuns in Winchester. Made entirely in gold laidwork on silk with stem-stitch outlines, these tiny embroideries are now fragile and faded, but their original effect would have been exquisitely colourful. Durham Cathedral.

Laidwork of a different kind was used on the Bayeux Tapestry, from which this head of Earl Harold comes. All the faces are in outline stitch (which is the same as stem stitch, but worked with the thread on the opposite side), but the hair on all the figures is without any detail, using two-ply crewel wool on linen. Bayeux Tapestry Museum, Normandy.

The face of a soldier from the fifteenth-century Guicciardini Quilt, made in Sicily. Every motif is executed in the stuffed-quilting technique where stuffing is introduced from the back of the embroidery after the outlines are stitched in back stitch. The spaces between the motifs are worked in close rows of running stitch. Metropolitan Museum of Art, New York.

A man's head from a seventeenth-century raised-work panel from the Burrell Collection in Glasgow. The face is padded satin, but the natural curls are interesting, and appear to be a pattern of circles applied to the rest of the upper hair, overlapping the collar and shoulders.

Two fourteenth-century saints from an English altar frontal worked in 1315–1335. Here, lines of split stitch are packed closely together to suggest a very convincing sheen to the contours of the skin. The hair is a marvel of decorative waves very much in the style of Celtic manuscripts of the eighth and ninth centuries. British Museum, London.

This woman's head is from the same source as the man shown bottom left on the previous page, although the hair is worked quite differently in luscious waves falling from the smooth crown. Like the man, her face is padded satin embroidered with silk. Burrell Collection, Glasgow.

The head of a female saint from a cope of 1430–1460, worked in silk threads in split stitch to follow the flowing tresses of the hair. This creates a beautiful sheen, especially when highlighted with lines of couched gold thread. Victoria and Albert Museum, London.

A small simple head seen on a magnificent whitework sampler of 1664 made by Frances Cheyney. Cut and drawn work demands a more formal style than the realism of other techniques, but the clever use of needlepoint fillings and cutwork produces more of a pattern than a picture. Burrell Collection, Glasgow.

Crewelwork, using a two-ply crewel-wool thread on a linen-cotton twill, also has its limitations when only one colour is used throughout. In this detail from a biblical panel of c.1650, the hair is depicted in a series of waving single lines in stem stitch, with shading in straight stitch, back and running stitches, where every single stitch is shown up against the light background. Embroiderers' Guild Collection.

THE FACE

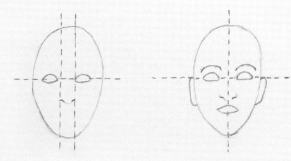

Eyes are set halfway down the head, with the width of one eye between them.

The tops of the ears are level with the eyes.

Men's ears are usually larger than those of women.

The distance between the end of the nose and the mouth will help to give some character to the portrait, as one millimetre can make all the difference between plainness and beauty.

The pupil just touches the top lid. The iris is partly hidden and rests on the lower lid.

The top lid has a fold when the eye is open. The lower lid is flatter than the top one, but this varies.

The beginning of the brow is usually on a level with the inside corner of the eye and set well above, but the space varies greatly. Male brows are usually heavier than those of females.

Eyebrows

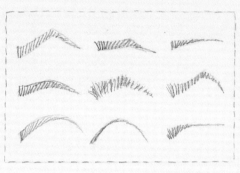

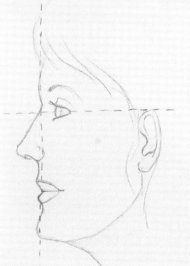

In profile, the eye resembles a letter A on its side.

For the purposes of small-scale embroidery, a backwards-facing letter C is usually adequate for the ear, worked in stem stitch.

The mouth seen from the side looks like this, and on a small scale can usually be made by stitches that form a sideways V.

Jawlines differ greatly; some are very pronounced, others are less visible, some angular, others rounded.

The throat in profile leaves the chin at a slope, rarely vertically, but double chins can be added for older people.

Female generalisations: delicate head; larger eyes and higher brows; small nose and full mouth; long, slender neck.

Male generalisations: heavier head and chin; more pronounced brow and longer ears; more muscular neck. Remember that in all types, the neck begins at the ears.

The hairline is important: too low over the brow tends to be unattractive. Study people's hairlines to see how they 'fit' differently round the head and ears and behind the neck, and notice how heads are different shapes too. Wrinkles add character to faces, as can double chins, folds, beards and bald heads.

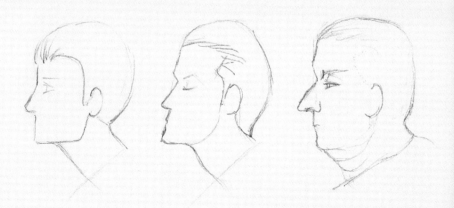

16

Individual features make all the difference to the character of a portrait and, although there is a limit to the detail possible on a very small scale, some attempt should be made to vary the shape of the head and face, the nose, eyes and mouth, depending on the age and gender of the subject.

THE BASIC HEAD

YOU WILL NEED

Closely woven, flesh-coloured cotton fabric

Matching sewing cotton

Sew-in Vilene, a non-woven interfacing

3mm (⅛in) thick padding, the kind used for quilting clothing

Stranded embroidery cotton for features and hair

Small pieces of felt for padding the hair

Amounts of materials needed will depend entirely on the size of your project. The worked examples shown here are no larger than approximately 3 x 2cm (1¼ x ¾in).

Note: The type of interfacing you choose for the face and neck is for you to decide, bearing in mind that the very firm weight is not easy to stitch through, especially with padding on top, and the softer weight is not easy to gather fabric round, as it bends instead of staying rigid. A good compromise is to use a firm weight for the head and a softer one, without padding, for the neck.

INSTRUCTIONS

1. For the basic head: cut one base from Vilene, using the pattern opposite. Cut five layers of the 3mm (⅛in) padding to the same shape, which should give a pile of about 1cm (½in) thickness.

Cut one oval shape from the flesh-coloured fabric, using the pattern, and run a gathering thread round as shown, starting and ending at the chin. (This will remind you which way up it is.)

Note: if you are making more than one face at the same time, Kay Dennis's easier alternative method of gathering the edge is to hold the uncut fabric in an embroidery hoop to keep it taut, marking the face shapes with a pencil. Run the gathering thread just inside these, about 4mm (⅛in), before cutting them out.

It seems to make no appreciable difference whether you cut the face on the cross or on the straight grain. However, the lacing across the back (step 2) should be done with care to avoid any folds of surplus fabric showing on the right side. So the smaller your gathering stitches, the easier this will be.

2. Place the padding, cut to shape, into the centre of the fabric with the Vilene on top, then draw up the gathering thread and lace across the back to draw in the folds and tighten the fabric on the right side. Fasten off securely. The right side will show a gentle curve; the back should be flat. The face is now ready to be embroidered.

Note: The face will be distorted if you embroider it before padding and lacing.

PADDED HEAD USING COTTON FABRIC

Scale the size up or down to suit your requirements.

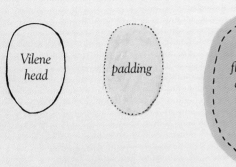

side view of
padded head

Note: the use of Vilene under the padding is to keep the contours of the face from sinking through to the back. It provides a firm surface for the indentations.

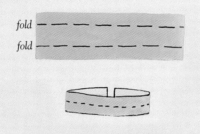

For ears, cut a fabric strip 5 x 1.5cm (2 x ½in).

Fold the long edges in towards the middle and sew them down with a running stitch. Fold the ends inwards and adjust to the width of the face, pin in place and press ends to flatten folds.

enlarged view of end of ear-strip

Stitch the ends of the ear-strip (not the middle), pushing the corners in between the two layers to make a curve.

ALTERNATIVE EARS

1. Cut a strip of Vilene with rounded ends, paint it pink and set this under the head as in the diagram opposite.

2. Work vertical satin stitches over the Vilene instead of painting it.

3. Cut a piece of felt in the shape of a large D to represent the ear, tuck the straight edge beneath the side of the head and sew it to the background all round. This last method is best for use with the felt heads as seen on page 72.

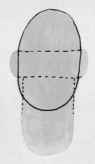

The ear-strip is set behind the head at the halfway point, the top of the ears level with the eyes. After securing the neck, sew the ear-strip down with matching thread, but do not stitch the visible parts of the ears to the background. When sewing the head over this, it is not necessary to sew through the ears.

Note: depending on the hair-style, it may not be necessary for your subject to have any ears.

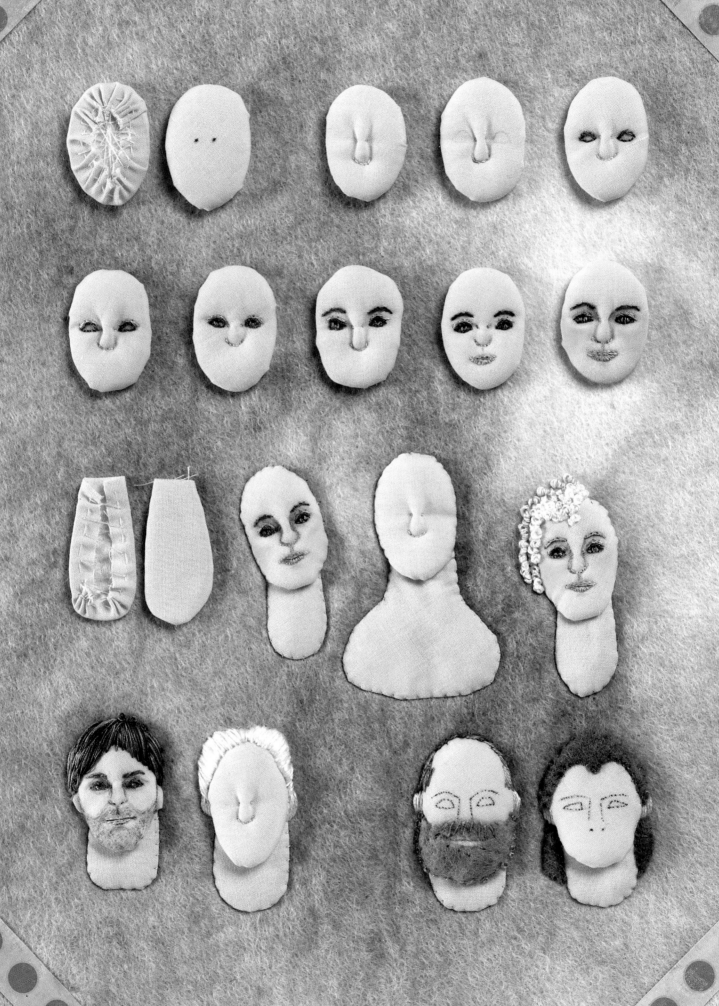

3. Halfway down the oval shape on the right side of the fabric, use a pencil to make two dots marking the bridge of the nose. This halfway mark is also the eye-line. Using a sewing thread, tie a knot in the end and take the needle through from back to front, coming up at one of the dots. Make a stitch through the padding from this dot to the next, pull firmly, and pinch the fabric to make the ridge of the nose. Pass the needle two or three times from one dot to the other under the surface, then out at the back. Now mark the base of the nose with four tiny stab stitches in the shape of a shallow U. Fasten off securely. This has the effect of pulling the two halves of the face together, which is why the eyes should not be marked until this is done.

4. Mark the eyes very lightly with either a sharp pencil or a gold gel pen. The distance between the eyes is critical, so leave a space of at least one eye-length between the two inner corners. Aim for an almond shape with the lower edge flatter than the upper lid.

5. Embroider the outline of the eye on the surface only, using a single thread and a tiny stem stitch for the upper lid and a back stitch for the lower edge.

6. Using a darker flesh-coloured thread, work two lines of stem stitch above the upper lid to add another dimension to the eye.

7. With your chosen eye colour, work satin stitches to form the iris, which should touch both the bottom and top lids. Then, use either black paint and a fine brush or a black drawing pen to make a single dot, representing the pupil. This should not be in the centre of the satin stitch but just below the top lid. The facial expression will depend on this placement. Alternatively, a tiny stitch of black thread will have a similar effect.

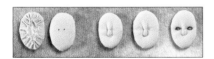

Shape of head with fabric gathered on reverse side, laced across. The nose is indented, the eyes marked, then outlined with tiny stitches.

A paler eyelid is added above the eye, the eye colour added, with the pupil, then the brows, lips and pencil-crayoned cheek colour.

The neck piece, laced across without padding. The head can be set at any angle over this, or it can be enlarged for a wide neckline. Hair may be added directly in simple French knots. The chin is left unstitched on all these samples.

Straight stitches in doubled random-dyed thread make a short hair-style over ears. Ears can be made in a matching colour of satin stitch, and the beard is made of brown felt, like the hair in the last sample.

8. Draw in the curved eyebrows, leaving a good space between each one and the top of the eye. Men's eyebrows tend to be heavier, lower down, and less shapely. Then embroider these on the surface, in stem stitch, using a single thread.

9. The mouth is embroidered in satin stitch for the lower (fuller) lip and stem stitch for the upper lip. Ideally, this should come halfway between the end of the nose and the chin, but variations in this detail can create a large or receding chin. I have used a very fine painted line (size 0 or 00 brush) to show the space between the lips.

10. A coloured pencil rubbed gently on to the cheeks to suggest contours, and a deep flesh-colour in the corners of the eyes and down the sides of the nose help to accentuate the features. Alternatively, paint may be used, but this should be applied sparingly, and fairly dry. (Use watercolour or gouache paints and very fine brushes.)

11. The neck is made by lacing a shaped piece of the same fabric over the Vilene, without a turning at the top, which is hidden beneath the head. The neck is sewn in place on the background before the head is applied. Usually, no padding is needed for the neck.

12. Keeping the head and neck separate allows the angle to be changed easily and keeps the chin free of the neck. The stitching is taken from where the face meets the neck, right round the top of the head to the neck on the other side. I find it useful to hold the head in place with a few spaced-out stitches before filling in the rest.

The photographs on these pages are enlarged versions of the images on the previous page, showing the stitching clearly.

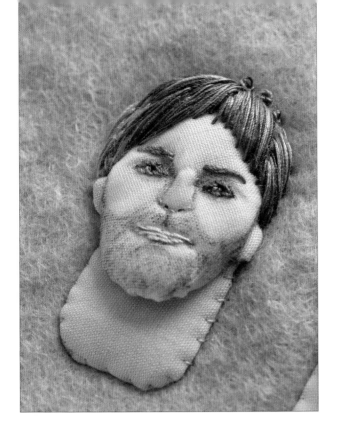

13. The neck shape can be enlarged to include the upper body, if this is to be seen in the finished portrait. It will be noticed that the face begins to curve as soon as it is sewn to the background.

14. Hair may be added directly on to the edges of the face at this point. The part-worked example shows French knots and bullion stitch using two strands of stranded cotton and two wraps round the needle, four for the bullion.

15. Men's necks are generally wider than women's and they tend to look shorter, too. So different versions are needed, depending on your character. On the four examples shown in the bottom row on page 20, a piece of shaped felt was used to bring the hair forward. From left to right: satin stitch worked over the felt in a variegated thread; receding hair in white, worked over white felt; a rough brown felt used to create a beard for a balding man, though this could also be covered in stitches, if preferred; longer hair made by three pieces of shaped felt sewn down with very tiny stitches closely packed.

Ears are discussed on page 19 and can be made in a variety of ways, either by sewing a narrow strip of fabric across the back of the head so that the ends project, or by cutting a piece of shaped Vilene and covering it with satin stitch. Some men's ears are very long, while ladies' ears tend to be daintier.

23

Miss Ringlets, seventeenth-century style.

Miss Victoria.

Miss Brown-Curls.

PAINTED FACES AND STITCHED HAIR-STYLES

A whole book could be written about this element alone, but the few examples on this and the following pages suggest ways in which a variety of stitches can be combined to make a convincing portrait, bearing in mind that the scale of your chosen materials must correspond to the style and size of the figure. A too-heavy thread or stitch can easily spoil the effect.

A note about the faces. These have all been painted using artists' watercolour and gouache (which is watercolour plus white), a very fine brush (size 0 to 000) and very little water. The fabric is a fine flesh-coloured cotton, so only the features are painted, apart from a faint trace of pink on the cheekbones which can be produced with a dry, coloured pencil. In most cases, but not all, certain features have been indented with a stab stitch taken through to the back, using flesh-coloured sewing thread: the corners of the eyes (both sides), the nostrils and the corners of the mouth. This is usually done after the head and neck are sewn in place on the background, though there is no reason why it can't be done beforehand, to allow for a second attempt. If your chosen hair-style covers the ears, these can be left off.

Note: the embroideries on pages 26–27 are shown actual size; those on pages 28–33 are enlarged for clarity.

24

The white-haired dowager.

Black-haired young lady.

Blonde chignon.

Ms Redhead.

Blonde princess.

The swept-up style is padded with a piece of felt cut to the shape of the hair. This is first stitched to a spare piece of calico, framed up on a small hoop, and covered with vertical lines of satin stitch. In this portrait, white and silver-grey thread was used, one strand of each used together.

Leaving an extra 3mm (⅛in) of fabric all round, cut the embroidered shape out and apply it to the head,

turning the allowance under and stitching it to the background and forehead with very small stitches. If gaps appear in the hair, these can be filled in with more satin stitches. Before closing the top of the head, you may wish to add more padding between the felt and the background fabric. This should be done sparingly, poking it in with a blunt needle. To neaten the edges, French knots are made to resemble tiny curls, and a coronet of pearls sits on top.

BLACK-HAIRED YOUNG LADY

BLONDE CHIGNON

This is a very simple style using a bought 'crinkly-synthetic' knitting yarn which is couched down in four or five lengths from one side of the head to the other. This yarn can be bought on-line and at haberdashery counters and craft stores in variety packs containing six or seven braids of the same colour.

As with the white-haired dowager, the hair was worked seperately over a felt base with stitches radiating from the face. Stem, split and straight stitches were used, with French knots to conceal the join. This style has the advantage of staying firmly in place, unlike the vertical satin stitch. The top of the hair is lightly padded, and the bun is worked over a small felt shape. Bullion knots below the ears suggest escaped tendrils.

This was worked directly on to the head and background, beginning with
a smooth satin stitch on the forehead and crown. A satin stitch roll above
this suggests a chignon. Bullion knots are worked randomly down each
side of the face, and French knots neaten the hairline. No padding was
used here, but the colour of the hair is improved when a random-dyed
thread is used, or two tones of the same colour (one strand of each).

Some knitting yarns of wool, synthetic or cotton, are so textured that, with a few twists, a bundle of hair is created instantly. The one used here is a highly twisted cotton gimp dyed randomly, bundled into a knot and held down with pins on top of the head, stab stitching into the strands to hold it in place. That's all. Slub yarns are useful for this, but some are too large to be used on this scale.

Another couched hair-style made up of two twisted bundles of silk slub yarn placed one on top of the other, stab stitched into place. Long, medium or short styles can also be created in this way.

MISS BROWN-CURLS

MISS VICTORIA

As this resembles a head of thick curls, the hair is made over a separate shape of brown felt covered in French knots and cut out before being applied to the head. By keeping all the French knots just inside the edge of the felt, the calico backing can be cut away close to the stitches, making turnings unnecessary. Extra French knots are then worked into the exposed edges. In this example, three strands of cotton were used, each in a different shade of brown, with three twists for each stitch.

To heighten this hair-style, a small crescent of felt was added to the top of the head over which straight stitches are taken to a centre parting. The hair can either disappear behind the ears, as it does here, or cover them. Loose ringlets are made as shown on page 64.

ANNE OF CLEVES

FROM SOURCE TO EMBROIDERY

This painted version of Anne of Cleves (above), fourth wife of King Henry VIII, is taken from the famous miniature painted by Hans Holbein in 1539. Although this version is fairly detailed, it could never do justice to the original which is a mere 4.5cm (1¾in) in diameter and exquisite in every respect. Even so, my 'copy' provides a useful starting point for deciding which parts would translate into appliqué, stitchery, beading and paint. A copy also helps to understand the construction of the costume (which is quite complex), and the nature of the ornament, and to see which parts should be laid down first and which could be left out or changed. Even a rough sketch will help to answer these questions.

On the painting, I left out the gold chain, but included it on the embroidery. Changes were made to the face, too, to balance the rich heaviness of the costume and, although my sitter now bears little resemblance to Anne of Cleves, the portrait reflects the foreign sumptuousness that her future unpredictable husband found so baffling.

THE EMBROIDERY

To prevent the background from showing through, the painted face and neck were backed with calico before being applied to the plain blue cotton. The head-dress was made in a separate piece on a small frame over a thin layer of padding sandwiched between two pieces of soft calico. This was embroidered with beads then cut out, the edges turned in, and applied over a shaped piece of white gauze to represent the veil. Extra beads were added along the hairline before the top of the veil was sewn in position.

The embroidery, shown actual size.

The dress, which looks more complicated than it is, is a series of gold collars applied over red cotton fabric, the outer one criss-crossed with gold thread and edged with couching, the inner one adorned with gold rings and beads. Holbein painted a full-length portrait of Anne at the same time as this miniature; time was not on his side, and a miniature was quicker. So there are slight differences in the details on the two portraits which have been incorporated into my design to make interpretation simpler.

Anne's love of gardening is reflected in the simple knot garden that surrounds the circle. Each section is a piece of cream patterned cotton, with the intersections filled with French knots. These were assembled on a separate piece of calico, then cut out and mounted over 0.5cm (¼in) thick foam board (easy to cut, clean, light, and available from art and large stationery shops). Thick gold braid covers the meeting of the two backgrounds.

The circle on the opposite side to the portrait represents another knot-garden motif quilted on calico with deep yellow seeding and back stitch. This was mounted over a circle of card applied with invisible stitches covered by French knots.

The folding cover was made to protect the delicate embroidery inside, the raised circle on the left (see opposite) fitting exactly into the depression containing the portrait. The calico squares lining the inside are in fact one long rectangle laced over two squares of card, allowing for a 1cm (½in) space between them. In each case, the embroidered sections are glued in place on top of this, with the protrait itself (which is actually a square) secured in place beforehand.

Anne's initials, AC, were embroidered in chain stitch and French knots on a rectangle of buff linen large enough to cover two more squares of card cut very slightly larger than the inner pieces. The outer cover was then laced over the cards with the spine

The surface of the circular surround is padded, making it higher than the portrait so that the quilted knot garden fits over the portrait exactly, as a kind of protection.

Tiny metal rings act as gold mounts for jewels, which are beads glued to painted discs of card.

down the centre and the corners neatened before sewing the inner and outer sections together all round. This is finished off with a thick gold cord. There is no fastening.

The swan and coronet emblem, applied gold kid and beads, represents Anne's house of Cleves.

PADDED HEADS IN PROFILE

INSTRUCTIONS

1. From Vilene, cut out the head shape, including the neck, and lay this on the bias-grain of the flesh-coloured cotton. Mark the shape all round very lightly with a pencil, then cut beyond this mark to leave an allowance of 1cm (½in). The padding comes later.

2. Lay the Vilene shape on the pencilled outline and hold it firmly to the fabric as you turn the edges in and stitch them down, keeping exactly to the shape of the head and carefully snipping towards the inside curves at nose, throat and back of neck. The turnings should be caught lightly on to the Vilene, but the needle and thread should not penetrate further than this. A running stitch can be taken from the back of the head over the top as far as the forehead to gather the fabric on to the curve, but all other parts are pleated and folded in, the generous allowance of 1cm (½in) making it easier to snip away excess fabric as it appears. For a closer fit over the bridge of the nose, pull excess fabric in with a secure stitch that does not show on the right side. Any raw edges that cannot be avoided, especially under the nose, can usually be neatened by a dab of white glue or Fray Stoppa.

3. Padding the profile head after covering the Vilene makes for a more accurate line all round. When the shape has been covered, cut a small hole (no larger than a pea) on the reverse side of the Vilene. Into the cavity between Vilene and fabric, insert flat pieces of padding to fill out the forehead, back of head, cheeks, chin and nose, with less towards the neck. Do not overpad, as this will become more obvious when the head is sewn to the background and pressed upwards from below (see step 5, below).

4. Paint or embroider the features as suggested in the diagrams below, then with flesh-coloured sewing thread make stab stitches into the corners of the eye just inside the bridge of the nose, and at the corner of the mouth. This will give an extra dimension to the surface.

5. Apply the head to the background and sew it down. The exact shade of sewing cotton, a fine needle, and very small stitches will help to make this appliqué almost invisible. Where stitches will show, they should be about 1mm (¹⁄₁₆in) apart. Small adjustments may be made at this stage, for instance by turning under the sharp point of the nose, and by pulling in the bridge of the nose more tightly.

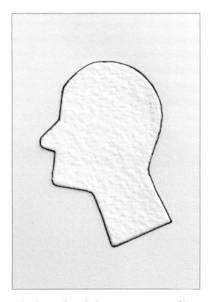

The basic head shape seen in profile.

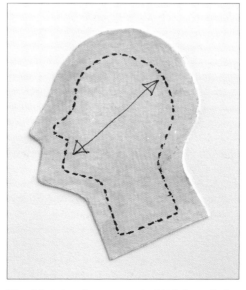

The fabric head-cover marked lightly with the shape, cut on the bias.

The embroideries on the facing page are shown actual size; those on pages 40–41 have been enlarged for clarity,

The profile head is not laced across the back like the full-face version. Each section of the covering fabric is folded inwards over the pencilled outline on the Vilene and stitched carefully on to the surface without penetrating the right side. Clipping should be done with caution. The hole on the reverse side shows where the padding will be inserted.

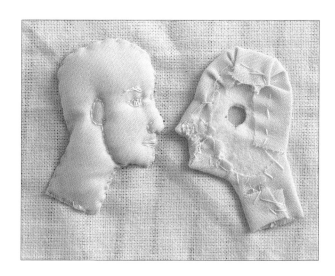

Long ringlets can be made using coloured wire, as in this sample. See page 64 for details. The smooth topline is made by satin stitch, the roll and bun over a piece of shaped Vilene.

The smooth hair is in stem stitch, but the rest is covered by a French hood fashionable in the year 1536. There are several varieties of this style, favoured by Anne Boleyn, Henry VIII's second queen. On this version, short lengths of ribbon were used for the hood.

The centre and back sections of hair are worked in satin stitch over a felt padding, including bullion stitch and French knots. Narrow braid is applied between these shapes.

A man wearing a Tudor bonnet over a short hair-style and beard worked in stem and straight stitch. Note how the stitches follow the direction of the hair growth.

A wig worked in chain stitch suggests a more textured surface adorned with rolls made of cotton-covered wire. As the wire was a different white from the embroidery thread, I painted it with gouache (watercolour mixed with white to make it opaque). The pigtail was made separately, the join concealed by a bow of black velvet ribbon.

WHITE EDWARDIAN LADY

Seen in profile, the Edwardian lady of *c.*1870 was worked entirely in white
fabrics and threads, relying on texture rather than colour to create the
interest. A broderie-anglaise cotton was used for both the background
and dress, although the former was 'knocked back' (embroiderers' term for
'subdued') with an overlay of plain cotton. Very fine and narrow bands of
bought lace work very well at the neckline and sleeves, with the cut edges
turned under before stitching.

Measurements: 19cm x 14.5cm (7½ x 5¾in)

THE DRAWING

A preliminary sketch taken from parts of photographs
helps to define the pose, the way the costume can be
layered, and the position of the figure within
the frame.

THE DIAGRAM

There are four main pattern pieces, the shaded areas
showing where one piece overlaps another.

a) head and neck
b) hair
c) body
d) sleeve, arm and hand

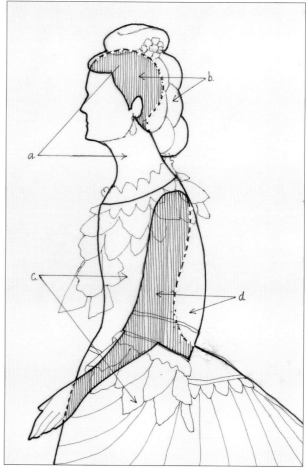

The hair is worked in satin stitch over a padding of white felt using an off-white stranded cotton. Note how the hairline curves over the forehead.

The arm/sleeve is made separately and stitched on at the required angle. The hand is quilted in one piece and added afterwards.

The images on these two pages are enlarged in order to show the stitching and materials used more clearly. The embroidery on page 43 is actual size.

On this scale, it is essential to use only the finest lace edgings, as anything too coarse will look wrong.

Posture is important. Edwardian ladies were notoriously elegant.

THREE-QUARTER HEADS

The three-quarter view may pose a few more problems than either the full-face or the profile, depending on the exact angle of the head and the complexity of the hair-style. Head-hugging styles and frilly caps are easy enough to show at any angle, whereas large picture hats and elaborate coiffures require more ingenuity to look convincing. In my samples, the features are both painted and embroidered.

In many cases, with the three-quarter view, an extension of felt will be needed from the nearest edge of the head to the back, surrounding the head like a crescent that disappears at the top of the far side. Ideally, this felt extension should be the same colour as the hair, stitched down with matching thread, then covered with embroidery.

Two basic three-quarter views are included, one slightly smaller and more rounded than the other, which shows a flatter side and a stronger chin. Both of them face to the left, but to reverse them, turn the template over. Whichever side you choose, mark the right side (R.S.) to remind you which way round it is, but remember that the R.S. will be covered by the padding and fabric, not the side that faces you as you lace across the back.

The neck template is the same for both heads and can be used either way round or upside down. In a three-quarter view, more of one side of the face is visible, and only one ear. So the centre/nose-line is well to one side, and all the features should be in line with this: eyes, nose, mouth, chin, hair-parting, etc.

Draw your face first to place everything in the correct position, noting where the ear will come and how much of the side and back hair will be seen. Check to see if any hair is visible on the far side of the face and, if so, whether it is level with the nearest side. If the hair is swept back off the face, no hair at all may be seen on the far side.

When setting the head on the neck, make sure that the neck reaches the ear on the visible side. It cannot stop short of this point. Move the head about on the neck to find the best position, but try not to have too much of the neck hidden behind the head as this makes more layers for the needle to pass through. If necessary, make a shorter neck. Having decided on the type of collar, remember that unless the face is turning to look over the shoulder, this will also be a three-quarter view.

STITCHING

The chin and jawline can be either left unstitched or stitched to the neck, but do not pull appliqué stitches too tightly as this may produce little bumps. They should, however, be placed very close together.

In the three-quarter view, it is more important than ever to place the appliqué stitches very close together, about 1mm ($\frac{1}{16}$in) apart, except where they will be covered by hair or garment. Sewing thread should be exactly the same colour as the face. If tiny puckers threaten to spoil a smooth edge, tease them away with the point of the needle and place stitches there to prevent them reappearing.

Once the pieces are stitched to the background, mark the hairline with a sharp pencil and paint the hair to match the felt extension (see diagram opposite). For the hair, use two tones of stranded cotton, one strand of each.

The samples shown on pages 48–49 are actual size. On pages 50–53 they are enlarged to enable the stitching to be seen more clearly .

   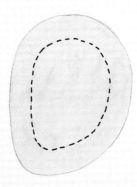

Two templates for the three-quarter view heads cut from firm Vilene, one smaller and more rounded than the other. The flesh-colour represents the cotton cover with the appropriate head marked on it, the gathering stitches to be placed nearer the cut edge with the layer of padding between Vilene and fabric. The neck needs no padding. These shapes are laced across the back before being stitched to the background, ready for the hair.

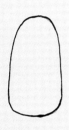 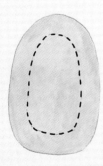  

The neck. Cut one from Vilene, with a fabric piece to cover it. If the costume covers the neck, a separate flesh-coloured neck will not be needed.

The head is set on the neck either way up, so that it meets the ear.

An extension like this may be needed to build up the hair and to raise the level to that of the padded face. Extra padding is not usually necessary unless the hair-style or hat is very large, like the mob-cap on page 50. The hair has been painted on to the pink fabric beyond the hairline, and now both this and the extension will be embroidered over, as seen in the examples on pages 48–49.

48

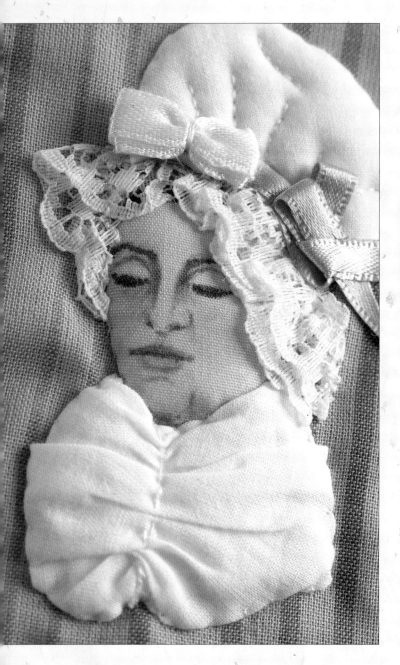

A padded mob-cap with a lace frill covers the hair.

The straight hair is embroidered in stem stitch over an extension of pale felt. Remember that when the hair falls over the shoulders like this, the garment must be sewn on before the hair is embroidered.

The straight stitches for the hair are taken across the extension from the hairline, leaving a space for the ear. Indoors, the elderly lady wears a tiny bunch of lace on her head, with a gathered lace collar.

French and bullion knots are worked over a brown felt extension. It is tempting to use a thicker thread for the knots, but in fact it is easier to pull two strands through the padding (Vilene) and felt than three or four.

STUART LADY WEARING A RUFF

The face is lightly padded beneath a double layer of chiffon with embroidered features and lightly painted cheeks. A coloured pencil will work equally well for this. The dark hair is also embroidered. The gold head-band is a crescent of gold kid held in place with fine metallic thread (Madeira Metallic no. 15, gold 22 behaves well in the needle). Above this is a red braid, then a crescent of blue felt with tiny diamanté jewels glued on. The neck and shoulders are in two pieces of fabric-covered Vilene (no padding) stitched to the background with a length of gathered lace for the ruff.

BEARDED MAN IN LILAC COAT

The face is lightly padded, the neck cut all-in-one with the face. The hair shape is applied felt covered by straight stitching using two strands of stranded cotton in two tones, lighter on top to suggest a three-dimensional effect. The face covering is a double layer of tea-coloured chiffon which stretches easily over the padding and Vilene base. It also quilts well. The features are embroidered in a single strand of stranded cotton with a very light application of watercolour paint in the eye socket. Unpadded felt is used for the coat, and white Vilene for the shirt with satin stitch worked over the collar.

MAN WITH A TRICORNE HAT AND WIG

VICTORIAN LADY

The Victorian lady has a lightly padded face with embroidered features over a cotton skin. Her hair has a padded felt extension at the back over which is worked a combination of straight, satin, stem and split stitches in a variegated grey stranded cotton.

The face is lightly padded under a double layer of skin-coloured chiffon, and the features embroidered using a back stitch stabbed through to the back and pulled to indent the eyes, nose and creases. The hair is knitted in two pieces using single moss stitch and a fine-textured yarn on size 3mm needles, suggesting the luxuriant curls of a shoulder-length wig. The coat is fabric-covered Vilene applied to the background, and the cravat is a piece of folded and gathered broderie anglaise. The tricorne hat was made by stitching felt to painted Vilene to make a single firm shape, round the top edge of which was stitched a textured white cotton yarn to suggest ostrich plume. Any white stitching that shows can be concealed by a dab of black paint. The hat is sewn down along the lower curve only, leaving the top free. Behind this is a piece of grey felt to represent the crown of the hat.

BESS OF HARDWICKE

This embroidery is based on a portrait of Bess of Hardwicke, Countess of Shrewsbury, who became a wealthy land and property owner in Derbyshire during the reign of Elizabeth I, and was at one time on friendly terms with Mary Queen of Scots, whose captivity was the responsibility of Bess's husband.

The portrait is worked in straight stitches, French knots and woven wheels, with some chain stitch round the edge of the ruff. The background is calico, with the stitches following the direction of the facial contours and the play of light upon the skin, allowing none of the background to show through.

For the frame, a cut-out rectangle of card was laid over the portrait and stitched with satin stitches on to the calico, finished off with a couched gold cord and tiny gold studs at each corner. To complete, another frame of gold card was placed on the outer edge, before setting the completed piece on a 'wallet' of patterned card that folds across the portrait.

The tightly curling hair is made of closely packed French knots and woven wheels using a variety of tones in orange-brown. Although tedious to stitch, the ruff had to be precise in both shape and shading to achieve the exactness that typified Bess of Hardwicke. Apparently, she and her last husband (number four) fell out a great deal, as she did with her large and fractured family, but she was a truly fascinating woman whose home at Hardwicke Hall in Derbyshire still stands, complete with furnishings and her own embroideries. It is maintained by the National Trust.

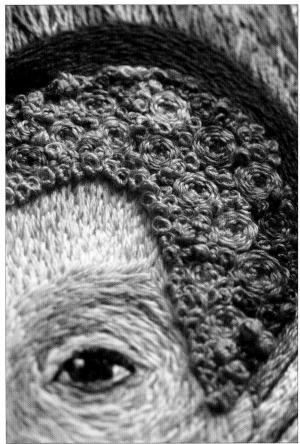

Appliqué hands

You will need

Tracing paper or baking parchment
Soft calico for the foundation
Pink cotton fabric for the covering
Stiff sew-in Vilene
Padding, 4mm (⅛in) thick
Cord or smooth string no thicker than 1mm (1⁄16in)
Needle, matching thread and tacking thread
Small sharp scissors
Glue stick and fabric glue
Embroidery hoop (optional)
Watercolour paints and fine brush
Cocktail stick

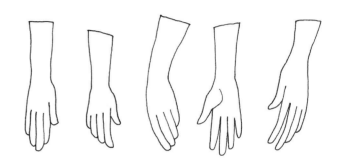

Instructions

The following steps are shown on the opposite page:

a) Trace the hand shape and transfer it accurately on to a piece of Vilene. For the opposite hand, turn the tracing over. Cut the Vilene out with sharp scissors.

Place the Vilene hand on the calico and tack it down with a few stitches. Leave a space of at least 2cm (¾in) between hands, if you are making more than one.

b) From the tip of each finger to the wrist, lay lengths of cord and glue these in place. Press the cords down until they are fixed and, when the glue has dried, take a few stitches over the top to keep them there. Keep all 'holding stitches' within the Vilene shape and avoid snipping them during the final trimming.

c) Cut a piece of padding to cover the arm and wrist, leaving the fingers bare. Stitch this in place.

d) Tack a piece of pink covering fabric over this, as shown, and begin to quilt the hand using very small back stitches, pressing the fabric between the cords to indent each finger. By pressing the fabric on to the cord as you go, the outline will easily be seen. The fingers should be of an even thickness.

e) Keeping just to the outside of the stitches, cut the hand out.

f) Trim away as much as possible without cutting into the stitch lines. Using the pointed end of a cocktail stick, smear the cut edge all round with fabric glue, pressing down any frayed edges with your finger. Leave this to dry. To give an even smoother appearance, use paint to cover the fabric on the outer edge of the hand, matching the background colour exactly. Do not paint the stitch line.

g) The hand is glued in place on the costume, after which you may need to go round the edge again with matching paint to cover any pink gaps. These worked examples show open and closed hands in which the fingers are kept together.

Drawings of hands in various positions are shown above.

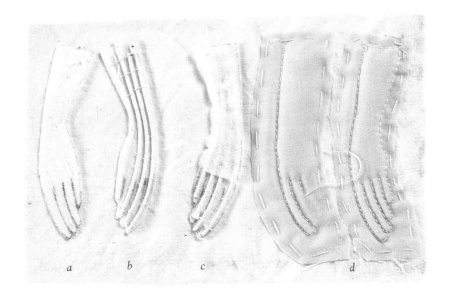

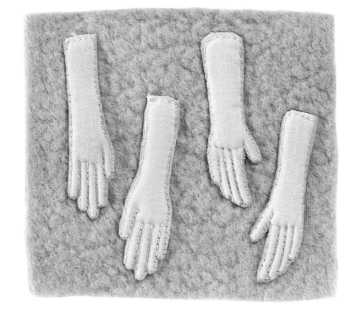

STITCHES FOR HAIR

An embroidered portrait can easily be spoilt by the unimaginative and clumsy depiction of hair, which should be a major element in the composition. The scale of the thread and stitches is vitally important and should reflect the size and style of the 'sitter'; a too-coarse stitch or thread will look more Rastafarian than Vidal Sasoon, and although a detailed hair-style will probably take longer to make, the result will be well worth the effort.

STITCHES

Satin, long and short, straight, stem, split, chain or any combination of these are useful stitches for smooth hair. For knotty hair, use any knot stitch, raised chain, raised stem or couched threads that have a textured look, though some textured knitting yarns may have to be 'sheared'. Needleweaving on a small scale also suggests 'wild' hair. For curls and waves, try woven wheels, French knots and bullion knots, and couched cords. Instead of taking the needle through to the reverse side, stitches can sometimes be worked entirely on the surface.

THREADS

These should be scaled down to suit the size of the head. One or (at the most) two strands of stranded cotton is usually fine enough for the small heads shown here, or even one strand of sewing cotton or silk. It is usually much easier to pull one or two strands through fabric, padding and Vilene than to pull through three or four. Heavy threads and yarns are usually the wrong scale unless you can pull them to pieces. Silk imparts an attractive sheen, and the addition of metallic threads and beads highlights the styling.

COLOURS

Since hair is usually a mixture of many different tones, the use of two tones in the needle often gives a more lively realism than one flat colour. I usually have three or four tones of the same colour available to give even more permutations. Variegated threads are excellent for this purpose. Use a single strand doubled over so that the colours mix more unevenly. Whip lines of stitches with another tone or colour for more subtle colour mixing.

Observe hair colours and see where the tones fade and change, streaks, highlights, grey-white near the ears and brow, etc. These changes add more life and individuality to a portrait.

Soft curls are couched over cords with beads in the spaces. In the centre, chain stitch makes a sleek texture. On the right, knitted gold mesh and gold cord is couched over a pad of yellow felt, with added beads.

Free-flowing hair can be suggested by waves of straight stitch using a random-dyed stranded cotton.

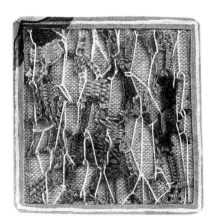
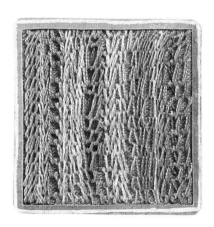

The samples shown here are actual size. On pages 58 and 60–61, the samples are enlarged for clarity.

Curls at the top are suggested by woven wheels over seven and nine spokes with French knots between. The waves are couched stranded cotton worked over shapes of thick Vilene kept in position with a dab of glue.

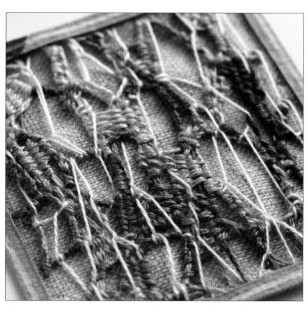

Unkempt hair can be created by free-style needleweaving, either with random-dyed threads or several tones overlaid. Tiny beads will add to the effect. Worked over a sparkling or shimmer fabric, the effect would be stunning.

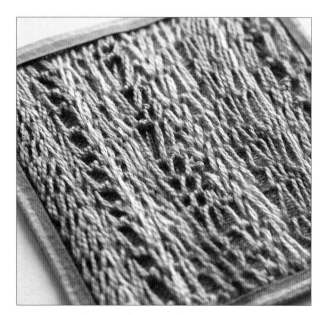

Long crimpy hair can be created by any straight stitch in closed lines, but this sample uses both raised stem and raised chain band. Knot stitches would produce an interesting effect too.

Tight curls of bullion stitch can resemble braids, plaits, rows of ringlets or a beard. For contrast, Bokhara couching resembles combed ridges.

Herringbone stitch suggests finely plaited hair.

Chain stitch whipped in both directions adds another layer of colour and texture. This could also be used for fine plaits.

Whipped stitch.

Knot stitch.

MAKING CURLS AND RINGLETS, PLAITS AND OTHER THINGS

Convincing ringlets and rolls for wigs can be made in several ways using threads and wire. Wire can be bought either self-coloured or cotton-covered, on small reels or in straight packs (hanks). Even chenille sticks (pipe-cleaners) and craft equivalents, couched down, may be useful. Gold and silver wire of various thicknesses can be found on-line and in craft shops.

'Desire Memory' thread made by DMC is a wire covered with a fine satin thread that keeps its shape when bent. It comes in a range of colours including silver and gold. With this, one can make loose or tight ringlets.

The samples shown opposite are actual size. Above and on pages 64–65, the samples are enlarged for clarity.

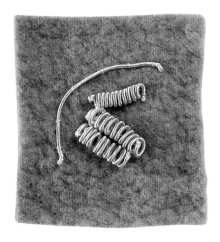
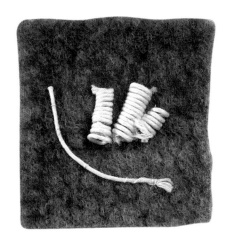

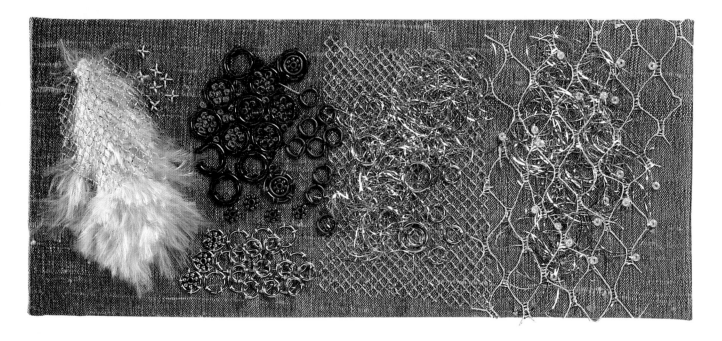
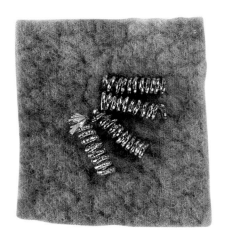

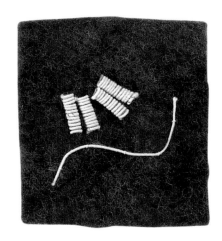

White cotton-covered wire in two different thicknesses makes good 'wig-curls' when coiled round cocktail or kebab sticks, a thick needle or a knitting needle.

Fine painted wire is sold on tiny bobbins in boxes of assorted colours, including copper, gold and silver, and is very easy to use. Larger tools make looser curls.

This is the hair used on Miss Victoria (page 33) made of stranded cotton soaked in diluted fabric glue, then wound round a piece of plastic drinking straw. When dry, this ringlet can easily be slid off by squeezing the straw.

Short lengths of fur fabric edging can be sheared to any density and used to represent hair. Partly covered by a mesh of gold, perhaps scattered with seed pearls, this can be made to look quite exotic.

Metal rings used for jewellery making can be used for stylised curls in combination with French knots and smaller rings. Gold rings laid over silver ones break up the pattern.

A fine mesh of gold is the background on which is stitched a mass of gold 'waste' (bought in small packets) decorated with gold rings in two sizes.

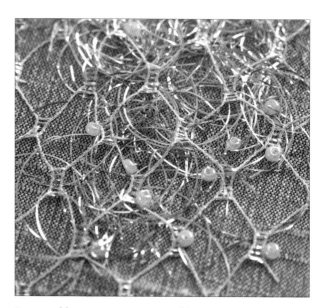

Loose golden tresses are suggested by an open gold mesh, gold 'waste' and creamy pearls. The background fabric showing through can add an extra dimension, especially if it is multi-coloured or patterned.

WIGS

This page of samples illustrates the use of knitting yarns (and a few chenille sticks) to create the kind of texture seen on wigs, some of which would also work well for natural hair. The choice of yarn is important, as anything thicker than the examples shown would be too heavy for a small face. I used 2 and 3mm knitting needles; finer gauges will produce a tighter texture. The more textured the yarn, the more the stitch pattern will be disguised, so smooth yarns call for a considered use of stitch. The ones I found most useful were simple garter stitch (every row knitted), reverse stocking stitch (the reverse side of stocking stitch, which has alternate knit and purl rows) and single moss stitch (every row k1, p1, on an odd number of stitches). A single rib is also useful (k1, p1, on an even number of stitches), and also a simple crochet stitch such as double crochet, half treble or treble.

A bouclé cotton yarn showing reverse stocking stitch.

A cotton slub showing the right side of stocking stitch.

A synthetic mohair knitted in single moss stitch.

The samples shown opposite are actual size. Above and on pages 68–69, the samples are enlarged for clarity.

A cotton bouclé with 'tails' of unspun yarn trapped in the base thread. These have been trimmed after knitting to produce a good untidy texture.

A random-dyed four-ply, knitted in single moss stitch, produces a good curl effect.

A synthetic mohair yarn with long ends sticking out of the base twist, knitted in reverse stocking stitch and trimmed to represent shaggy hair.

A similar yarn to that shown top right, with shiny silver-grey threads trimmed after knitting.

Chenille sticks are bent into a wig shape with the side pieces twisted round a kebab stick to make spirals. The cut ends are bent upwards with point-nosed pliers, and extra lengths can be sewn on to bulk up the sides.

A simple male wig is made of two separate lengths with the ends bent up to form curls.

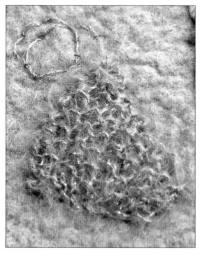

A fine one-ply mohair with glitter is knitted in garter stitch to make a convincing curling texture.

A two-ply variegated wool yarn knitted in single moss stitch breaks up the pattern.

A silver-grey embroidery cord knitted in single moss stitch for a special effect.

A grey four-ply wool crocheted in half trebles makes an interesting crimped texture.

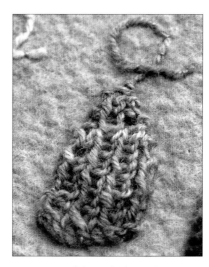

A variegated four-ply knitted in single rib.

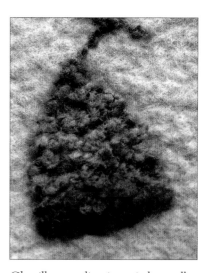

Chenille yarn disguises stitches well and softens the pattern. Knitted in garter stitch, this variegated yarn makes convincing hair, though any other stitch would work as well.

69

USING FELT

One of the main advantages of using felt on small-scale projects is that no turnings are necessary, as the fabric does not fray. So the shape can be cut to the exact size and sewn over a very light padding, with iron-on Vilene as a stabiliser. Felt is particularly useful on small complex shapes like the profile faces, for instance, but as the edges of felt can be unstable, care should be taken not to tear the finer points (chins, noses, fingers) away with the stitches by placing the latter too close to the edge. This is why Vilene is so useful (see below).

Note: it is inevitable that edge stitches will show, but the essential thing is that they should be placed evenly apart and be all the same size. If you prefer the appliqué stitches not to show, they can usually be hidden by an embroidery stitch worked over the top, or a couching thread, beads, a ribbon, band or cord.

Fine, closely constructed felts are best on small projects, but some of the thicker, rough types are useful for hair, beards, fur and clothing.

Paint does not work well on the fuzzy surface of felt, so the features are indicated by stitches alone. Several good skin-tones are available, but it is best to avoid any that are too highly coloured. Hand-dyed felts are also very useful, often bought at craft fairs in 10cm (4in) square bundles.

Felt can be used in conjunction with other fabrics too, for example cotton appliqué face with felt hair, beard or clothing; felt face with stitched hair or other hair methods; felt used as a padding instead of the usual wadding used for quilting, but note that when covering a padded face shape with felt, an extra allowance should be made to accommodate the 'bump'.

For head-dresses and clothing, felt often gives a padded appearance without the need for extra padding beneath. But take care that the parts of the portrait that should recede are not brought too far forward by the over-enthusiastic use of padding.

To give felt more stability, as for the tricorne hat, for instance, sew or iron it to a piece of Vilene cut to the same shape and painted with the same colour. Stitch all round (over the edges) and stitch through the Vilene when you apply it to the background. Other materials that don't fray are leather (real and fake), plastic-backed fabrics, papers and card.

TO MAKE A POINTED END WITH A BRAID THAT FRAYS

For braids and cords that refuse to be cut neatly, use Fray Stoppa (or similar) to soak the ends, then squeeze the fibres together with your fingers. Lay a length of matching thread along the braid near the end (sewing cotton is fine), leaving an end long enough to thread into a needle. Now start wrapping the cord with the rest, working towards the cut end and binding it tightly over the glued part until you get a point. Then hold it until the glue becomes tacky. The wrapping should come to about 1mm (1/16in) from the end. Leave enough of the thread to sew this end to the background before cutting it off. The other (beginning) end of the sewing thread can be finished off by stitching it into the braid. In a few moments, the wrapped point should be dry and firm enough to sew into place with more over-and-over stitches, the loose thread being used to sew the rest down.

The profile head is made in one piece, as shown below.

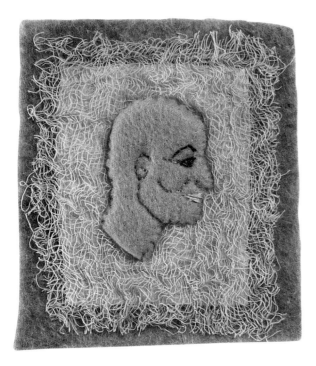

The full-face head (shown right) is made in two pieces, neck and head separately. The neck is not padded. The instructions are provided on the following page.

The samples shown here are actual size. On pages 72–73, the samples are enlarged for clarity.

Instructions for making the full-face head

1. Using the same pattern as for the fabric version (see page 19), cut a Vilene neck shape and attach this to the background with a few stitches.

2. Cut the same shape from felt and lay it on the Vilene, sewing it all round with a matching thread.

3. Cut a head shape from Vilene, padding and felt, remembering to leave a small allowance for the 'bump'. Attach the Vilene first, then the padding with a few securing stitches. Stitch the felt shape over the top of these, using the Vilene edge as a guide. If you are adding ears, they should be tucked in between the felt and the padding, as shown in the example. In this felt version, the chin is stitched to the neck.

4. The nose is made from a very small oblong of felt rolled up tightly into a long 'sausage' which can then be trimmed to fit. It is attached to the face with a few stitches taken from the reverse side, then pulled together at the bridge with a thread taken from side to side.

5. The eyes and mouth are embroidered. Indent the corners of the eyes and mouth, as with the fabric faces.

Draw the profile on to the Vilene, with the neck attached, and cut this out accurately. The expression and refinement of the features will be decided at this stage, depending on the cutting.

1. Lay the Vilene template on the felt and cut it out to the same shape, allowing an extra 2mm (⅛in) all round. Cut the padding to the same size as the Vilene.

2. Place the Vilene shape on the background and secure it with about 12 stitches. Place the padding on top and hold with a few more stitches which should not project beyond the Vilene.

3. The felt shape goes on top, held down with the thumb as tiny stitches are made through the edge, using the Vilene as a guide. Begin with the profile, where the stitches will be placed closer together than elsewhere. However, the felt and Vilene edges should be aligned all round to keep a good shape.

4. Mark the features in profile, using tiny back stitches.

NOTE:

The jawline is angled or curved towards the earlobe.

The ear is rather like a reversed C.

Indent the mouth at the corner and, using pink double-strand thread, make two straight stitches in a sideways V for the lips.

Indent the base of the nose. You may also wish to take a few stitches towards the corner of the mouth, but this is optional.

The eye in profile resembles a sideways A, with the cross-bar as the eye.

The brow is not indented but embroidered on the surface with very small stem stitches.

FELT HANDS

The best that can be done with felt hands is to make a mitten shape with the thumb attached, the material being too unstable to make separate fingers on this scale.

The images on this page are the actual size of the embroideries, and show how felts of different skin-tones can make a difference to the authenticity of the character. Exactly matching sewing threads are important too. The images on the right have been enlarged for clarity.

Small pieces of hand-dyed felt are useful for both hair and clothes, as colours are usually seen as combinations of tones, especially hair, which can sometimes appear to be striped. The use of stitched lines over felt provides a light-and-shade effect, as on the woman's longer straight hair, and a more ragged stitch suggests a feathery effect on the man's. Quick pencil sketches can provide a wealth of detail for small portraits; the position of the ear, the hair texture, the tilt of the nose, and so on.

Notice hand and finger positions too, and check that the thumb is in proportion to the fingers. A portrait can easily be spoiled by ugly hands.

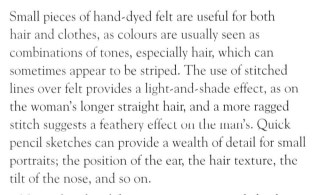

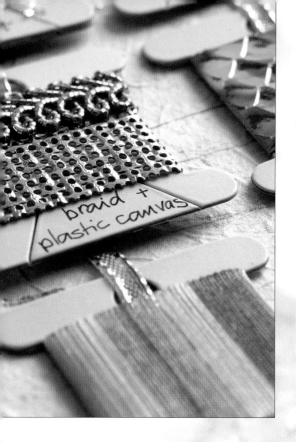

FABRICS LESS LIKELY TO FRAY

On a small scale, badly behaved fabrics (e.g. thick, springy, coarse or fraying) are best avoided. Materials for appliqué which will not usually fray are felt, leather, faux leather, Vilene and other non-woven interfacings, plastic-backed fabrics, tapes and bias-bindings, florists' wrappings, cords, papers and cards, though some of these may be tough to sew by hand. Also useful are ribbons which, although fraying at the cut ends, can successfully be sewn together, edge to edge, to cover small shapes. Florists' ribbon, some with wired edges, are useful too as they are less likely to fray than some others.

Iron-on Vilene will help to prevent most fabrics from fraying badly. Fray Stoppa is a glue specially intended for use on fraying materials but, as this may leave a dark mark, it should be applied with caution. White craft adhesive works well and dries invisibly. Cottons backed with iron-on Vilene are good for small pieces, the finer the better, although some heavily printed fabrics are difficult to penetrate with a hand-held needle.

The best cottons are those with a woven-in pattern, or dyed, also broderie anglaise and other machine-embroidered cottons. The criterion here, as with all other patterned fabrics, is the scale of the pattern, which should be in keeping with the size of the portrait. However, here is an opportunity to use those precious scraps you've been saving for a small project.

On this page are shown samples of fabrics that either do not fray, or fray less than others. Even the gold net can be 'stopped' at the edges.

embellished lace net

embroidered net

"knitted" net

embroidered net

machine lace

silver net

plasticised fabric

gold net

sequined jersey-knit

real + faux leather

braid + plastic canvas

plastic "leather"

thick felt

ribbon

hand-dyed felt

paper

organza ribbon

florists' ribbon

CLOTHING THE PORTRAIT

Since all my sitters are well-behaved and aware that their likeness is being recorded for all time, they wear their finest clothes and present few problems of position. Full-face, profile, or three-quarter views only (let's keep it simple). Consequently, the only kind of challenge presented by the clothing is likely to be in the choice of fabric and the amount of detail you can achieve in the space available. The latter, of course, is up to you, but I have chosen to avoid all legs either by hiding them under skirts or by cutting off the portrait at chest- or waist-height like the miniatures of the Tudor and Stuart eras. (There was an unknown portraitist of this period known as the 'Master of the Half-Lengths', for obvious reasons.) So the clothing need only consist of the bodice and sleeves, at most, with collars, ruffs, jewellery and head-wear to add interest. Not even hands need be shown, unless you wish it.

On the opposite page are seen some samples of finer fabrics useful for small-scale projects because of their construction and pattern.

machine lace

chiffons

stripes

printed
cottons

nets and
edgings

plain
cottons
and
linens

Striped fabrics can suggest the direction of the garment, a sleeve angle, a collar, etc. Stripes also make interesting borders, either down the stripe or across it, but remember that the reverse side of the fabric may be just as useful as the right side.

Metallic lace tends to unravel on the cut edges unless the loose strands are held down securely with plenty of tiny stitches, preferably using the same or similar metal thread. As with cotton lace, it looks best when another interesting fabric shows beneath.

Chiffons and other 'see-throughs' are invaluable for either intensifying the colour beneath it or reducing it. Some useful chiffons are 'shot' with contrasting colours or speckled with metallic stars and spots. Some might fray badly so, when turning edges under, use a matching backing fabric to prevent the turnings from showing on the right side.

The frayed edges of roughly woven hand-dyed muslins can suggest the texture of hair or clothing, as once the fibres are stitched down they behave quite well. Printed cottons are invaluable, but the patterns should be chosen with care as anything too large will be out of scale.

BASIC BODICE AND SLEEVES

1. From a drawing or photograph, trace the basic shapes of the bodice and sleeves and transfer these to a stiff paper template (pattern) to keep as a reference.

2. Use the paper template to transfer the shapes to a medium-weight Vilene, and cut these out for use on the embroidery.

3. Pin the Vilene shapes to the reverse side of your chosen fabric, taking care to centre the pattern where possible.

4. Leaving an allowance of at least 7mm (¼in) all round, cut out the patterned fabric, then turn the allowance over on to the reverse side using the edge of the Vilene shape as a guide. Clip inside curves and gather outer curves. Tack these in place as shown top left on the facing page and enlarged below. These pieces are now ready to assemble.

5. Stitch the neck and head in place before arranging the bodice in position. The face and hair will usually have been embroidered before you do this.

6. Cut out the bodice and sleeve shapes in thin wadding and place these under each fabric shape, then position the neckline of the bodice to cover the lower edge of the neck, pin in place, tack, then attach to the background with very small stitches in a matching sewing thread (shown top right opposite and enlarged on page 85).

The samples shown here are actual size. On page 82 and pages 84–85, the samples are enlarged for clarity.

This is the basic appliqué procedure for making a front-facing portrait which can be adapted to any fashion by changing the fabric, the neckline or the sleeves. Padding is a matter of personal preference.

The bodice shown bottom left on the previous page and at the top of the facing page shows how an embroidered net has been laid over a foundation of printed cotton. The net is tacked into position after sewing the foundation layer on to the Vilene, then removing the tacking stitches. (If you should accidently leave these in, they will become trapped between the two layers.)

In the bodice shown bottom right on the previous page and at the bottom of the facing page, a wide machine-embroidered cotton edging has been used for the bodice and skirt, with a narrower lace border to finish off the neckline and extend the sleeves. The lower neckline in this embroidery exposes more skin, but the extended neck can sometimes be a difficult shape to cover without wrinkling. One solution is to divide the Vilene neck and chest by a curve (where a necklace would be) and to cover each piece separately with the skin-toned fabric cut on the bias. These are then placed back together again and sewn down, the join being hidden by a pearl or jewelled necklace or velvet choker. You may prefer not to pad the neck and chest area.

The fabric used for the bodice shown top right on page 83 and below was striped alternately with a lace pattern and sprigs of flowers, but for the bodice and sleeves, only the lace panels were used.

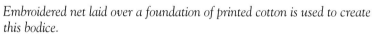

Embroidered net laid over a foundation of printed cotton is used to create this bodice.

In this example, a wide machine-embroidered cotton edging has been used for the bodice and skirt, with a narrower lace border to finish off the neckline and extend the sleeves.

BASIC GARMENTS IN PROFILE

Usually, only two main garment shapes are seen in profile, the top of the
bodice and the shoulder part of the sleeve which overlaps it. The method
of working is the same as for the full-face figure, with the choice of
neckline being a factor at the head-making stage. As before, the head and
neck should be embroidered first and applied to the background before
the clothing shapes are cut out, as tiny measurements may change in the
process. Padding the costume pieces is optional: you will see from the
three examples on the facing page that the one on the left is padded, the
centre figure has no padding in the sleeve, and the one on the right is not
padded at all, the relief being caused only by the folded-under fabric and
slightly stiffer Vilene.

*The samples shown opposite are actual size. Those shown
below are enlarged for clarity.*

a) Basic head with short neck. The top of the shoulder (if seen) will be covered by the garment fabric.

b) Basic head with lower neckline in which the top of the shoulder, if seen, may need to be covered with skin fabric.

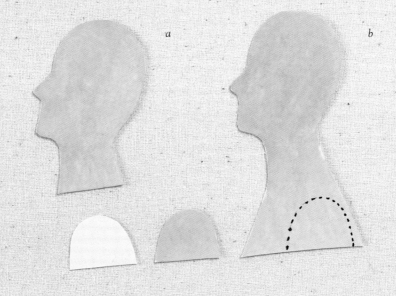

A high neckline can easily be reshaped from round to V-shape by the addition of a braid. The direction of the stripes indicates the position of the arms, and padding may not be necessary.

The high cravat covers the short neck, and the jacket collar is cut all-in-one with the bodice. It is faced on the reverse side with the same fabric.

A low-neck style may have sleeves or straps only.

Postcard portraits

Early studio photographs in sepia brown or tones of grey make an excellent subject for a series of embroidered portraits, perhaps of the family, where the background is often little more than a faded curtain or a shadowy wall. Some of these old photographs were small, but mine are the standard postcard size: 6 x 4in (15.2 x 10.2cm). The background can be either left to fade away on the edges, or bound with strips of matching fabric, as with Mr and Mrs Arbuthnot shown on pages 90 and 91. Any paint used on the background looks better if it fades away gently like the photograph rather than messy lines which have no meaning.

There are various methods of constructing embroidered postcards, depending on the technique you choose, but my postcards are made up of two separate pieces of card (measuring the same postcard size) which should be firm but not too thick. These two pieces are covered on one side with fabric – embroidery on one card, plain calico on the other – then laced across before being sewn together, back to back, to make a postcard of the correct thickness with all the turnings hidden inside. (Having spent so much care on the front, I like the backs of my cards to show the same degree of finish, but this is a personal choice.)

For my two sepia-toned cards, I dyed my calico with tea and a quick spray of walnut ink while it was still wet. Each piece of dyed calico measured 20.5 x 15.5cm (8 x 6in) before making up and was tacked to a backing of muslin before embroidery began so that it would fit the embroidery frame as I worked. The exact shape of the postcard is marked out on the top (dyed) piece by drawing round a postcard template on the reverse side with a pencil, then tacking through the pencil lines in a contrasting thread. This will appear on the right side, without any of the pencil markings showing, and will ensure that the portrait sits inside the postcard area in the correct position. It also ensures that, if you need to alter the placing of the portrait at any stage, no pencil marks will show on the right side.

For the embroidery, any suitably fine thread can be used in tones of sepia, cream and near-white to match the colours of an old, faded photograph. For a black-and-white version, grey, charcoal and near-white are used. Be very sparing with black.

Make a sketch of your portrait, then trace the head and body shapes and transfer these to Vilene and fabric as previously explained, with a thin layer of padding between them. Embroider and sew all garments to the background before attaching the face, hair and hat, as the head will almost certainly overlap the neck. Position them very carefully inside the postcard shape before you sew. To check, it often helps to highlight any odd angles by holding the postcard in front of a mirror.

For the unbound version

The diagram opposite shows how the spare fabric covering the cards is folded over to the back and laced across to give an exact postcard measurement. The two pieces are then placed back to back and sewn together neatly all round the edges with a stitch known as antique seam, which pulls the two pieces together. These stitches are best placed no more than 3mm (⅛in) apart.

For the bound version

The diagram on page 89 shows how the edges of the portrait are extended by strips of matching fabric, each piece being folded inwards and pressed before being attached by hand to the portrait edge. Do this on the two short edges first, overlapping them by the two longer edges next. The spare fabric is folded over to the back and laced, just as in the unbound version. You may have to trim away some of the bulk on the corners before you sew them, but don't overdo this!

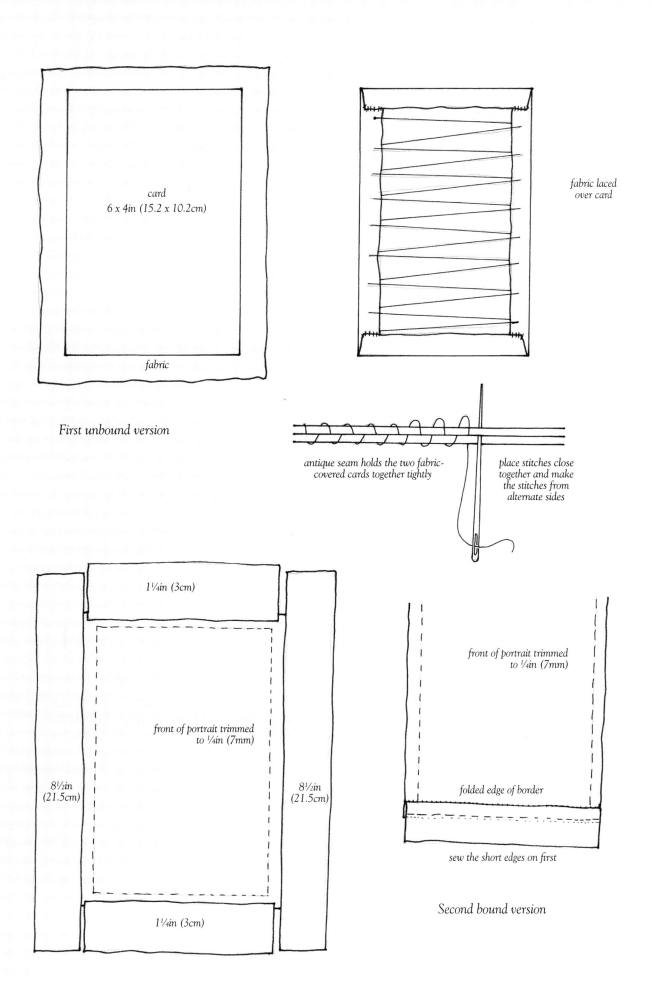

card
6 x 4in (15.2 x 10.2cm)

fabric

*fabric laced
over card*

First unbound version

*antique seam holds the two fabric-
covered cards together tightly*

*place stitches close
together and make
the stitches from
alternate sides*

1¼in (3cm)

*front of portrait trimmed
to ¼in (7mm)*

8½in
(21.5cm)

8½in
(21.5cm)

1¼in (3cm)

*front of portrait trimmed
to ¼in (7mm)*

folded edge of border

sew the short edges on first

Second bound version

MRS ARBUTHNOT

The face was worked before the head was applied to the background, the straight stitches for the hair added afterwards to cover most of the applied stitches.

The body is slightly raised with a layer of white felt, then fine white cotton fabric, then with pieces of shaped lace at each side of a striped ribbon and lace strip to suggest a blouse. This is embellished with tiny seed pearls. The neck-band is two ruched strips of lace, and the feather boa is a crochet chain of textured (trimmed) knitting yarn. The brim of the hat consists of overlapping layers of buttonhole stitch (two strands of linen thread), stem stitch and French knots.

THE DECORATION

Assorted beads of glass, wood, plastic and shell.

Leaf shapes cut from Vilene (painted) and embroidered with veins of fly stitch.

Flower shapes cut from Vilene, painted and stitched over with beads in the centre.

Tall feathers, lines drawn in first, embroidered from the top with overlapping fly stitch and fine chain stitch.

MR ARBUTHNOT

A tracing was made of the face and head, and this was used as the pattern for the paler fabric cut with a 0.5cm (¼in) allowance, and for the Vilene shape. Between these two pieces was placed a single layer of padding before lacing the fabric across the back. The features were painted and embroidered, as with his wife, before being applied to the background. The shirt front, waistcoat and jacket lapels are worked in satin stitch and Bayeux stitch before the head-piece was applied. With the head applied, the hair and beard were added to cover all appliqué stitches. Two strands of stranded cotton were used for this, using two different tones in the needle at the same time. In all, three tones were used.

The embroidered portraits, shown actual size, with enlarged details.

91

ONCE UPON A TIME

Papier-mâché boxes of all shapes and sizes can be found on-line and in the larger craft shops and at craft fairs, and with only a little imagination can be made into containers for postcard-sized portraits. The book-box shown here is about 2.5cm (1in) deep with a lip on the inside lid that fits the body of the book. It is painted with various tones of gold and silver acrylic paints, both inside and out. The lettering on the front cover was drawn on to card, cut out with a craft knife, painted (edges too), and glued down.

The portraits are worked inside the box and, for Prince Charming and Cinderella respectively, measure 8.5 x 13.5cm (3½ x 5¼in) and 10 x 14cm (4 x 5½in).

Each portrait is laced over card (with a light padding between) which should be measured accurately to allow for the thickness of the fabric to be turned over to the reverse side. If there is a gap, a braid or cord may be inserted and glued in place with the join at one of the bottom corners where it will show least.

Some research into period costume is always necessary, as the details can make all the difference to small-scale portraits. Prince Charming wears a bag-wig, where the tail of the wig is enclosed in a black velvet bag and tied in a bow to prevent the white powder marking his collar. The background to this portrait is a colour-washed cotton overlaid with a printed network of gold.

Cinderella wears a typically exaggerated powdered wig in eighteenth-century style decorated with a cut-out lace motif. Her dress is of layers of coloured lace over a background fabric of gold bead-studded net and brown shot silk. Both faces are painted and embroidered.

Cinderella's hair is a mass of textured knitting yarn sewn down with stab stitches, lengthened by cotton ringlets stiffened with diluted glue and wrapped round drinking straws (see page 64 for this method). Held in place with matching stitches, the ringlets blend into the wig on both sides without a noticeable join.

The high stand-up collar was a feature of men's coats at this time, enclosing a frilled cravat that fell down the open front. A striped silk collar extends from a metallic-silk fabric coat with a separate sleeve, and metal studs for buttons. His wig is stitched over padding, with two sausage-curls formed over felt-covered straws sewn down with satin stitch.

Old lace can be reused to add extra interest to all parts of historic costume. Jewels scattered in hair and wigs were quite usual, as were feathers of immense proportions, combs, ribbons and bows.

Beads are carefully chosen for both colour and size to edge the neckline and open bodice. This was the age of 'stomachers', those V-shaped inserts beneath the bodice that were often highly decorated with embroidery and laced across. Some gemstones are self-adhesive, like those used for the necklace, and gold jewellery 'findings' make a good basis for composite pieces.

STITCHES

The diagrams below and on the facing page show some of the stitches used in the previous portraits as well as some others that may be suitable. The most important factor to remember is that they should be worked to the same scale as the design. The smaller the design, the smaller the stitch and thickness of thread. Use any stitch that gives the texture and pattern most suitable for the purpose, even if it is not one 'in the book'.

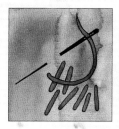

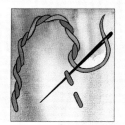

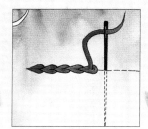

Straight stitch is made at random either close together or spread apart.

Whipped running stitch is made on a foundation of running stitches which are then 'whipped' with another thread, either in the same colour or a contrasting one. This gives a fine corded line.

Stem stitch is made diagonally to produce an accurate line of overlapping stitches.

Split stitch is worked in a similar way to stem stitch except that the point of the needle comes up through the centre of the previous stitch to split the thread. This is the most accurate of all line stitches.

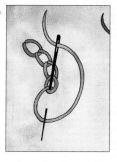

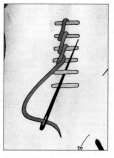

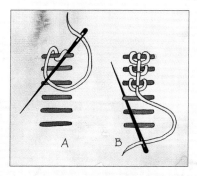

Chain stitch is worked towards you from top to bottom.

Twisted chain is worked in a similar way to chain stitch except that the needle is inserted outside the loop to form a twist.

Raised stem is stem stitch worked on a foundation of bars. The needle does not pierce the fabric except to begin and end the stitch.

Raised chain is worked in two stages to create a chain on a foundation of bars. As with raised stem, the needle does not pierce the fabric except to begin and end the stitch, and the bars may be of the same or contrasting colours as the chain.

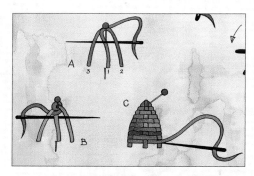

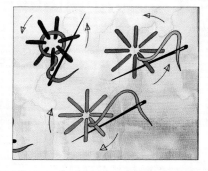

Woven picots make tiny triangles of weaving which, when packed close together, can look like points of hair. They can also be used for feathers and lace collars.

Woven wheels and spiders' webs. The woven wheel is made on an odd number of spokes and is worked from the centre outwards using the same colour or a contrasting one. The other two wheels are based on any number of spokes, one of them producing a ridged effect, the other smooth. They make good curls for hair.

Some more stitches that will be found to be useful.

Couching is a versatile stitch that serves many purposes, either with an invisible holding stitch or one that provides a contrast. Bokhara couching is an excellent filling stitch.

Long and short stitch is particularly good for shading and, in satin stitch, the shape can be raised and more clearly defined by working over a Vilene shape or thin card painted to match the thread. Good for hair, collars, cuffs, buttons, etc.

French knots are indispensable for tightly curled hair. Scattered between beads, it makes a sumptuous filling.

Bullion knots make wonderful curls. Used with a random-dyed thread and worked in all directions, the effect can be lively and textural. Used formally in rows or blocks, it takes on the character of a woven fabric or basketwork.

Herringbone is excellent for holding down applied pieces of fabric to prevent raw edges from unravelling. It is both decorative and practical.

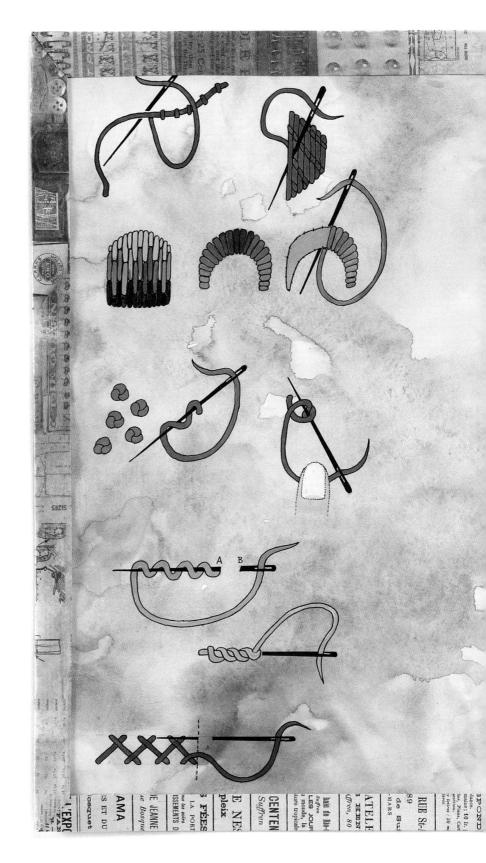

In couching, a thread or yarn is held down by a small stitch to make a line. Placed close together, lines of couching make a good filling.

Bokhara couching uses the same thread for both laid and holding stitches to produce a pattern, usually of diagonal lines.

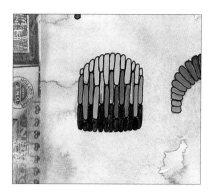

Long and short stitch interlocks to make a smooth filling which can show varying tones useful for hair and shading.

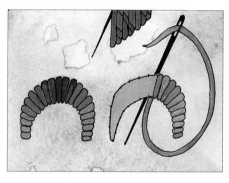

In satin stitch, the thread can be laid parallel or like this, following a shape. It can also be worked over a pad to lift the shape into higher relief.

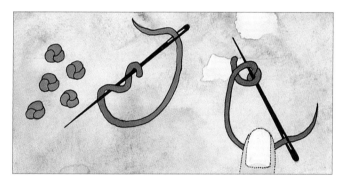

French knots are made by wrapping the thread round the needle two or three times. Hold the thread with the left hand to slide the 'wraps' towards the point, then steer the point of the needle to enter the fabric at the side of where the thread emerges, pulling the rest of the thread taut as you do so. Push the needle through the fabric whilst holding the wraps in place with one finger (yes, you can do this with only two hands!).

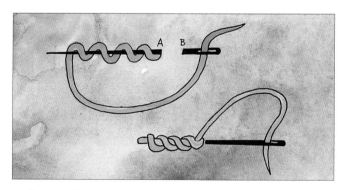

Bullion stitch. Bring the needle out at A, then insert it again at B and A but, before pulling the thread through, twist it several times round the needle point as shown. Keep these twists in place with your thumb, then draw the needle through both fabric and twists at the same time, sliding them down into a coil. Now insert the needle again at B so that the coils lie across the gap between A and B.

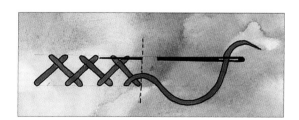

Herringbone stitch can be worked from right to left, or left to right. The stitches can also be worked closer together to make a more solid line. It can also be whipped.

INSPIRATION

As with clothes and hair-styles, perceptions of beauty have changed over time, and from country to country. Artists have usually reflected these changes by exaggerating features, often to the point of stylisation, making their work rich in ideas for embroiderers. From very earliest times, unknown artists and sculptors have blended realism with the contemporary notion that beauty was synonymous with goodness, perhaps thereby making it easier for the 'common man' to identify those characters who undoubtedly paid the eager-to-please artist or sculptor. Nowadays, we tend to accept realism, sometimes harsh, as a risk to be taken in sitting for a portrait, whether photographed or painted. But I imagine that, in Ancient Egypt, for instance, no such risk was contemplated by the sculptor, fresco painter or sarcophagus maker who wished to live to tell the tale. A far cry, we might say, from Oliver Cromwell's instructions for 'warts and all'.

Moving away from realism towards more stylistic conventions, we are able at once to identify particular features as being typically Egyptian or Japanese, Minoan or Indian and, in our own time, as 'post-Edwardian' or Art Deco. Instantly, individuality is sacrificed to a style which, as embroiderers, we latch on to as a few steps nearer to appliqué, quilting, hand or machine stitchery. Suddenly, it becomes a simpler process to aim for a certain 'look' rather than a more exact likeness to a painting or photograph of a real person, and it is this kind of simplification that can become a perfect introduction to the embroidered portrait.

Enlarged versions of the stitching on the sample opposite, inspired by the art of Ancient Egypt.

beard

collar

pattern on dress

Gustav Klimt

The Austrian-born artist Gustav Klimt (1862–1918) is a favourite source of decoration for embroiderers. His images of women's figures and faces often float upon a sea of rich geometric patterns, motifs and colours, cords and chiffon layers, some of which are influenced by the art of Ancient Egypt and the Spanish painter Velasquez, for example. In my sketchbook, I attempted to reproduce the well-known triangles using various simple embroidery techniques, and to pick out other motifs in preparation for a sample composition.

I identify a selection of mostly patterned fabrics that will help. I draw out the main shapes, eliminate others, and decide to place my figure within an asymmetrical frame more in keeping with Klimt's own arrangements than a plain rectangle. The small panel shown here measures only 20 x 15 cm (8 x 6in) and is mostly appliqué, hand stitchery and beading. I usually back my applied pieces with iron-on Vilene and sew them down with herringbone stitch which then becomes part of the decoration.

Pieces of textured gold leather, gold braid, printed fabric, French knots, beads and a metal ring are included in this triangle, outlined with gold cord. The eye motif was one that Klimt used often in his paintings.

Lightly quilted, this triangle is decorated with spirals of finely couched threads and seeding in a random-dyed cotton. All the stitching is done by hand.

Triangles of various sizes are stitched to a fabric background, the spaces between, all triangles, are filled with a needlelace stitch in random-dyed stranded cottons. Worked over bars, especially those of a different colour, this stitch covers the plain fabric beneath. A gold fibre-pen was used to mark the scrolls on the leather.

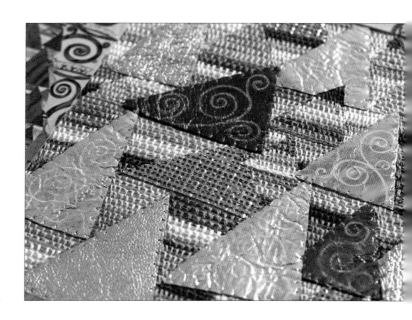

Left: another sketchbook page of Klimt-inspired patterns is a collage of paint sketches, drawings, paper and printed fabrics which identify many of the most attractive elements, the sumptuous colours, the ingenious use of pattern and the stylised pose of his sitters.

Above: my initial diagram for a small sample embroidery, seen on the next page, with some of the fabrics, mostly cottons, and a distressed silk for the background. Some simplification was needed to make Klimt's design suitable for stitchery and, even then, my first attempt was almost entirely pulled out before the second one began to work.

THE EMBROIDERY

Using matching colours, herringbone stitch was used to secure each piece of fabric to the background, except for the felt face, neck and hands which were first stitched, then outlined with chain stitch. Herringbone is especially useful for dealing with the messy edges of gold mesh, as can be seen in the details shown on this page. The long 'ribbons' of beads were first strung on to double thread then couched down along the curves, with added adhesive gems between. Heavy beading was used on the choker and bracelets, and the gold ovals were cut from foil, indented with a scroll pattern using an old dried-up biro.

The finished embroidery, shown opposite, is reproduced actual size. The details on this page are enlarged for clarity.

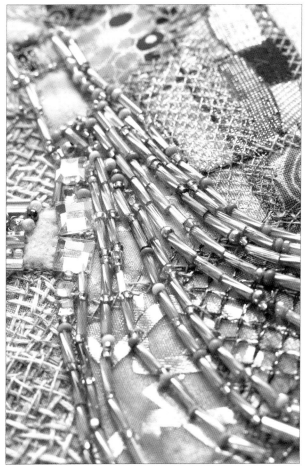

JAPANESE ART

Japanese art offers a wealth of decorative material that has long been
a favourite with western embroiderers, as the Japanese have their own
tradition of exquisite hand embroidery that decorates the exotic gowns
of the women in the portraits. In a different way, the men's costumes are
just as interesting and exciting, particularly the incredible suits of armour
made up of many small flexible parts laced together in complex patterns.
The men's helmets are a miracle of design, and the women's hair-styles
are beautiful and varied, and would make a rewarding study for a series of
detailed portraits using sumptuous gold and jewels.

Another sketchbook page identifies favourite elements and gives one a chance to sample techniques that might be useful in the embroidery, bringing together fabrics, colours and patterns as well as any printed inspirational material. In this case, hexagonal and log-cabin patchwork and quilting, together with the ubiquitous tassels, seemed like a promising first direction. The portrait below is seen as the actual size, in which I used a woven braid in the border, gold Christmas ribbon on the shoulders, gold lace over black felt for the hair, with various metal beads and ornaments.

HISTORICAL PORTRAITS:
AN INSPIRED COLLECTION

Portraits of the Renaissance period are, on my scrapbook pages, placed alongside those of a later French origin, some of which are by Erté, the Russian-born fashion designer who worked mostly in Paris during the early 1900s. Others are by Mucha, whose style of graphic art is usually recognised as being part fantasy and part fashion. On these pages, anything and everything can be done with hair and head-dresses, the more fanciful the better, some confections of lace and lawn, some bejewelled and plaited, some coiled and capped, braided and crimped.

Other possible sources of stylised portraits are:

Playing cards. Make drawings of these from a variety of packs and extrapolate the best bits for a series of detailed portraits with or without the mirror image.

Minoan frescoes from Ancient Crete, with very distinctive and alluring hair-styles.

Ancient Assyrian sculptures show marvellour hair- and beard-styles.

Byzantine mosaics, very rich and colourful. Greek and Coptic icons, too.

Celtic book illustration, which show beautifully simplified figures.

POSTCARD BOOK

Sometimes ideas germinate in what appears to be infertile ground only to grow, if we wait, into projects that excite and intrigue. This is what happened whenever I saw the ring-bound 'book' of manila envelopes in a craft shop, knowing that somehow it was telling me to use it. Eventually, I bought it, unblemished, new and crisp. Too good to use, of course. Some time later, a kind friend presented me with a bag of old lace bits that her grandmother had kept for many years. Some lengths were still in their original wrappers, French and English, with prices from the early 1900s, bias-binding too, old lacy collars and crocheted corners, white and blonde, fine and coarse, narrow and wide. Some bits were wrapped round pieces of card, one of which was a stiff, brown envelope addressed to a long-gone relative. The stamp dated it to the reign of George V, though there was no more to go on but his portrait. The two tokens inside told her that, if she presented them at the photographer's studio by a certain date, she could have five free black-and-white portraits. Obviously, she did not take up the offer but wrapped lace round it instead. It was much too personal for me to throw away.

I took out my envelope book. The old one fitted perfectly inside. My book had found its reason. The pictures on the following pages show what it looks like now, aged prematurely and tied with one of the lace edgings. So the first thing I did was to distress the envelopes to the same colour and shabbiness of the original, easily done by 'scrubbing' watercolour paint round the edges and, while the envelopes were still damp, scrunching them gently to make creases and dog-eared corners. They were then flattened out and allowed to dry.

Front cover

Back cover

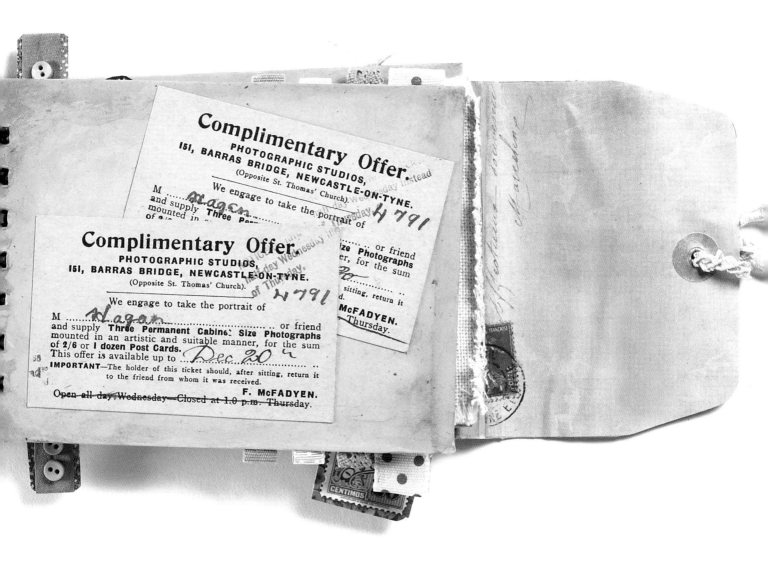

On the first pages, I stuck the old envelope
and the tokens in place as, once the book
has fulfilled its purpose, it will be returned
to its donor.

The first portrait, hatted in the style of that era, was embroidered in black and grey stranded cotton on a white linen background, suitably demure, as all sitters seemed to be in those days. Also decorating the page are typical ribbons, a pottery button and a label from one of the lace bundles with its price in francs.

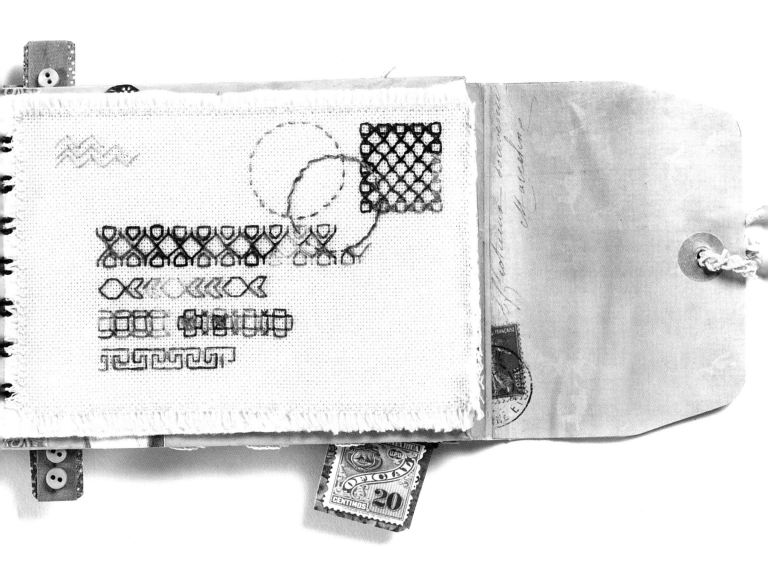

Opposite the portrait, rows of blackwork stitches give the impression of an address and stamp on an envelope, worked in a dark variegated thread. Torn, white paper beneath gives a more solid white than the brown envelope would have done. The rose on the flap is cut from a piece of patterned paper.

Using several of the paper wrappings, which I thought too evocative to throw away, I made a collage that includes drawings of hats from the period, which also give one a reminder of the severe hair-styles from the 1900s. Cloche hats, straight flat-fronted jackets, kid gloves and sensible shoes would complete the look.

The discoloured circle used here as a frame is from a card 'drum' for 18 yards (approximately 16.5m) of bias-binding. The Arcadian makers might have been interested to know that we still use bias-binding in the twenty-first century.

Hopping backwards in time, these drawings of white cotton bonnets show what was being worn in the country in the 1800s. Trimmed with handmade lace, they could have been made at home and worn with spotted muslins or block-printed cottons. Used on an embroidered portrait, these bonnets could frame a young face as attractively as in the lady's portrait on page 50.

An interesting way of framing a portrait is by using a related textile technique, as these examples show. Here, drawings from the 1820s and 1830s on paper are used in a part-worked patchwork, still with tackings in place. Borders and labels hanging outside the pages add another dimension to the experience of turning the envelopes.

Even further back in time, well before photography and free tokens, the lady from Jarrow might have had Tudor ancestors when miniature portraits were carried in lockets around the neck or placed in exquisite folding frames amongst private letters in a drawer. The earliest of these miniature gems by such artists as Holbein and Hilliard always had a bright blue background, like the Anne of Cleves portrait on page 35, and the sitter would usually be portrayed from the front. This small Tudor portrait shows the jewelled 'bilament' over a velvet hood, and a high frilled collar over a dress of needlelace stitch. Beads and fancy gold braid are used on the appliqué head-dress over hair worked in straight stitch.

Still on the theme of letters and portraits, the last page shows a collage of matching fabrics and handwriting, concluding with the words 'Read between the lines', a saying that may have originated when, to save paper and the cost of carriage, words were written both horizontally and vertically on the same side. In Tudor times, however, a colourful portrait may have said as much as words, and a postcard book of portraits would, as now, have made a very acceptable gift.

INDEX

Ancient Egypt 100–101
Anne Boleyn 40
Anne of Cleves 34–37, 126
appliqué 8, 11, 34, 38, 46, 56–57, 70, 76, 84, 91, 100, 103, 126
Art Deco 100

Bayeux Tapestry 10, 14
beading 34, 35, 36, 37, 58, 90, 95, 98, 103, 105, 111
beards 16, 21, 23, 41, 52, 60, 70, 91, 93, 112, 126
Berlin woolwork 10
Bess of Hardwicke 54–55
blackwork 12, 121
bodice 78, 82–85, 86, 87, 95
bonnets 41, 124
book-box 92–95
braid 29, 36, 41, 52, 70, 87, 93, 103, 111, 126

canvaswork 11, 12
chin 16, 18, 21, 22, 38, 46, 72
Cinderella 6, 92, 93–95
clothes (garments) 8, 75, 78–85, 86–87, 88, 100
coat 52, 53, 94
collar 11, 14, 36, 46, 51, 52, 78, 80, 87, 93, 94, 97, 98, 116, 126
cord 37, 55, 56, 58, 69, 70, 76, 93, 102, 103
couching 15, 29, 32, 36, 55, 58, 60, 98, 99, 103, 105
    Bokhara couching 60, 98, 99
cravat 53, 87, 94
crewelwork 8, 15
cutwork 15

drawing (sketching) 6, 10, 11–15, 22, 34, 42, 46, 56, 73, 75, 82, 88, 90, 92, 103, 105, 112, 122, 124, 125
dress 36, 42, 93, 126

ears 16, 19, 21, 23, 24, 46, 72, 73
Edwardian lady 42–45
Elizabeth I 11, 54
eyebrows 16, 21, 22, 73
eyes 16, 17, 19, 21, 22, 24, 38, 46, 53, 72, 73

fabrics 76–77, 78–81
    broderie anglaise 42, 53, 76
    calico 28, 33, 35, 36, 54, 55, 56, 88
    chiffon 52, 53, 81, 102
    cotton 18, 19, 24, 35, 36, 38, 42, 47, 53, 56, 76–77, 80, 81, 84, 85, 90, 93, 105, 124
    kid 37, 52
    leather 70, 76–77, 103
    linen 12, 14, 15, 36, 90, 120
    muslin 81, 88, 124
    net 76, 84, 85, 93
    satin 11, 14, 15
    silk 11, 14, 93, 105
faces 16–17
    appliqué 8, 70
    embroidered 10, 14, 15, 51–53, 93
    felt 70, 71–73
    full-face 18–23, 72
    padded 14, 15, 70

painted 12, 24–33, 34–36, 50–53, 93
    profile 39–41, 70, 73
    three-quarter view 46–53
Frances Cheyney 15

garments see clothes
goldwork 10
Guicciardini Quilt 14
Gustav Klimt 102–107

hair 46, 70, 97, 98, 99, 108
    curls 14, 28, 33, 53, 55, 58, 60, 62–65, 68, 69, 94, 97, 98
    felt 21, 70, 75
    knitted 68–69
    padding for 46, 47
    ringlets 33, 40, 60, 62–65, 94
    stitches for 58–65
    stitched 11, 14, 15, 16, 21, 23, 24–33, 40, 41, 44, 50–53, 55, 70, 75, 91, 94, 126
hands 8, 42, 44, 56–57, 74–75, 105
Hans Holbein 34, 36, 126
hats 8, 46, 47, 53, 70, 88, 90, 120, 122
head-dresses 35, 70, 112, 126
heads 8, 13–15, 16–17, 82, 8, 87, 88, 90–91
    felt 70–75
    full-face 18–23, 71–72
    padded 19–23, 28, 38–41
    profile 38–41, 71, 73–75, 87
    three-quarter view 46–53
Henry VIII 34, 40

inspiration 100–115

jacket 87, 91, 122
Japanese art 100, 108–111
jewellery 36, 52, 78, 84, 95, 107, 108, 112, 126

knitting yarn 29, 31, 53, 58, 66–69, 90, 94, 99
knot garden 36
knot stitch 58, 60, 61
    bullion knots 11, 23, 29, 30, 41, 51, 58, 60, 98, 99
    French knots 21, 23, 28, 29, 30, 33, 36, 41, 51, 54, 55, 58, 60, 65, 90, 98, 99, 103

lace 42, 45, 50, 51, 52, 80, 84, 90, 93, 95, 111, 112, 116, 120, 124
laidwork 14
looped purl 11

mob-cap 47, 50
mouth 16, 17, 22, 24, 38, 46, 72, 73

neck 16, 18, 19, 21, 22, 23, 24, 35, 38, 42, 46, 47, 52, 71, 72, 73, 82, 84, 86, 87, 88, 107, 126
needleweaving 58, 60
nose 16, 17, 21, 22, 38, 46, 53, 70, 72, 73, 75

or nué 12

painting 19, 21, 36, 41, 47, 53, 56, 70, 88, 90, 92, 98, 116 see also faces, painted
patchwork 111, 125
pigtail 41
plaits 60, 61, 62–65, 112
postcard book 6, 116–127
postcard portraits 88–91, 92–95
Prince Charming 6, 92, 93–94

Quaker Tapestry 12
quilting 18, 36, 44, 52, 56, 70, 100, 103, 111

raised work 8, 12, 14
Renaissance period 112–115
ribbon 40, 41, 70, 76–77, 90, 95, 111, 120
ruff 52, 54, 55, 78

saints 10, 14, 15
scrapbook 112–113
seeding 36, 103
shirt 52, 91
sketchbook 102, 104–105, 110–111
sleeves 42, 44, 78, 80, 82–85, 86, 87, 94
slub yarn 31, 32, 66
stitches 8, 12, 24, 34, 96–99
    antique seam 88, 89
    back stitch 11, 14, 15, 21, 36, 53, 56, 73
    Bayeux stitch 12, 91
    buttonhole stitch 90
    chain stitch 36, 41, 54, 58, 61, 90, 97, 105
    fly stitch 90
    for hair 58–61
    herringbone stitch 61, 98, 99, 103, 105
    long and short stitch 58, 98, 99
    needlelace stitch 103, 126
    outline stitch 14
    raised chain stitch 58, 60, 97
    raised stem stitch 58, 60, 97
    running stitch 14, 15, 19, 38, 97
    satin stitch 19, 21, 22, 23, 28, 29, 30, 40, 41, 44, 52, 53, 55, 58, 91, 94, 98, 99
    spiders' web 97
    split stitch 14, 15, 29, 53, 58, 97
    stab stitch 21, 24, 31, 32, 38, 94
    stem stitch 11, 14, 15, 16, 21, 22, 29, 40, 41, 50, 53, 58, 73, 90, 97
    straight stitch 15, 21, 29, 33, 41, 51, 52, 53, 54, 58, 60, 73, 90, 97, 126
    twisted chain stitch 97
    whipped stitch 61, 97
    woven picots 97
    woven wheels 54, 55, 58, 97
stuffed quilting 14
threads 58
    gold thread 10, 12, 15, 36
    metal thread 11, 52, 58, 80
    random-dyed thread 21, 30, 58, 60, 68, 98, 103
    sewing cotton 18, 38, 58, 70
    silk thread 10, 11, 12, 15, 58
    stranded cotton 18, 23, 33, 44, 46, 52, 53, 58, 60, 64, 91, 94, 103, 120
    variegated thread 23, 58, 69
Vilene 18, 19, 22, 23, 38, 40, 47, 51, 52, 53, 56, 58, 60, 70, 72, 73, 76, 82, 84, 86, 88, 90, 91, 98, 103

waistcoat 91
whitework 15
wigs 41, 53, 62, 64, 66–69, 93, 94, 95
William Morris 12
wire 40, 41, 62, 64, 76
wool 11, 14, 15, 31, 69